SmartHelp For Good 'n' Angry Kids

SmartHelp For Good 'n' Angry Kids

Teaching Children to Manage Anger

Frank Jacobelli and Lynn Ann Watson

WILEY-BLACKWELL
A John Wiley & Sons, Ltd., Publication

This edition first published 2009
© 2009 John Wiley & Sons Ltd.

Wiley-Blackwell is an imprint of John Wiley & Sons, formed by the merger of Wiley's global Scientific, Technical, and Medical business with Blackwell Publishing.

Registered Office
John Wiley & Sons Ltd, The Atrium, Southern Gate, Chichester, West Sussex, PO19 8SQ, UK

Editorial Offices
The Atrium, Southern Gate, Chichester, West Sussex, PO19 8SQ, UK
9600 Garsington Road, Oxford, OX4 2DQ, UK
350 Main Street, Malden, MA 02148-5020, USA

For details of our global editorial offices, for customer services, and for information about how to apply for permission to reuse the copyright material in this book please see our website at www.wiley.com/wiley-blackwell.

The right of Frank Jacobelli and Lynn Watson to be identified as the authors of this work has been asserted in accordance with the Copyright, Designs and Patents Act 1988.

All rights reserved. No part of this publication may be reproduced, stored in a retrieval system, or transmitted, in any form or by any means, electronic, mechanical, photocopying, recording or otherwise, except as permitted by the UK Copyright, Designs and Patents Act 1988, without the prior permission of the publisher.

Wiley also publishes its books in a variety of electronic formats. Some content that appears in print may not be available in electronic books.

Designations used by companies to distinguish their products are often claimed as trademarks. All brand names and product names used in this book are trade names, service marks, trademarks or registered trademarks of their respective owners. The publisher is not associated with any product or vendor mentioned in this book. This publication is designed to provide accurate and authoritative information in regard to the subject matter covered. It is sold on the understanding that the publisher is not engaged in rendering professional services. If professional advice or other expert assistance is required, the services of a competent professional should be sought.

Library of Congress Cataloging-in-Publication Data

Jacobelli, Frank.
  Smarthelp for good 'n' angry kids : teaching children to manage anger / Frank Jacobelli and Lynn Ann Watson.
     p. cm.
  Includes bibliographical references and index.
  ISBN 978-0-470-75802-1
  1. Anger in children. 2. Attitude change in children. 3. Child rearing. I. Watson, Lynn Ann. II. Title.
  BF723.A4J33 2009
  248.8'45—dc22

2008052789

A catalogue record for this book is available from the British Library.

Set in Scala and Scala Sans 10/13pt by Laserwords Private Limited, Chennai, India

Printed in Singapore by Fabulous Printers Pte Ltd

1 2009

*For Margaret Rose and Barbara Ann, for loving so well
and making so much possible*

No book, including this one, can replace the services of a qualified health professional. Please use this book to teach your child to improve his or her behavior, and to help you in communicating with your child's doctor and/or mental health professional so you and your child can obtain the best care possible. If you suspect your child's behavior or thought process is a danger to himself/herself or someone else, seek medical attention for your child without delay.

Contents

About the Authors   xi

Foreword   xiii

Acknowledgments   xv

1. Introducing SmartHelp for Good 'n' Angry Kids   1
2. Making Sense of Anger   5
3. Major Theories about Anger: A Brief, Annotated Guide   15
4. Character: Factory Installed or Add-On Equipment?   19
5. The Labeling of Children: When Anger Leads to Diagnosis   29
6. Reaching and Teaching the Angry Child—And How to Stay Sane in the Process   39
7. Learning Styles and Why They Matter   51
8. Kaytlin, Thomas, Lena, and Manny: A Few of Our Angry Kids   57
9. Before You Begin   73

Workbook A   Logical-Mathematical   **79**
    This Thing Called Anger   81
    Me in the Mirror   83
    Walt Learns to Wait   85
    Figuring Out Who I Am   87
    Crack the Cool Code   89
    Bonnie Can Balance   91

Workbook B   Bodily-Kinesthetic   **93**
    Snack-Food for Thought   95
    Frank Feels the Fire   97
    Counting to Calm   99
    Rockhound Rhonda   101
    Don't Blow It   103
    Paul Hits the Wall   105

Workbook C Intrapersonal — **107**
- Brenda in a Bag — 109
- Ray on the Rise — 111
- My Three Favorite Things — 113
- Color You Calm — 115
- When Gary Gets Going — 117
- Ben Beats the Blahs — 119

Workbook D Interpersonal — **121**
- Sizzling Simon — 123
- 'I,' 'I,' Irene — 125
- Hannah Asks for Help — 127
- Mirroring Matthew — 129
- Playing It Cool — 131
- Chuck Checks It Out — 133

Workbook E Musical-Rhythmic — **135**
- Larry's Lyrics to Live By — 137
- Rappin' Randy Raps It Out — 139
- Bobby Keeps the Beat — 141
- Sam's Secret Saying — 143
- Rockin' Ricky — 145
- Shake It Out Your Shoes — 147

Workbook F Visual-Spatial — **149**
- Mike's Magic Bike — 151
- What Bugs You? — 153
- Putting Feelings to Faces — 155
- The Train that Could — 157
- Vinnie on Video — 159
- Picture This — 161

Workbook G Verbal-Linguistic — **163**
- 'All or Nothing' Alex — 165
- Have a Talk With Yourself — 167
- Keep it Simple, Sam — 169
- Sarah Says 'I'm Sorry' — 171
- What I Really Mean to Say — 173
- Carla's Cool Friend Connie — 175

Workbook H Naturalist — **177**
- Tip of the Iceberg — 179
- Andrea's Ant Hill — 181
- Spencer in Space — 183
- Vic, the Volcano — 185
- Stella Sees Stars — 187
- Felicia Finds the Forest — 189

Appendix 1	Survey, Scoring page, and Graph—Eight Strengths Survey	**191**
Appendix 2	Answer Guide	**195**

Bibliography   199

Index   203

About the Authors

Frank Jacobelli has treated children, adults, and families in a variety of clinical settings including private practice, community mental health, and inpatient psychiatric. He is an adjunct professor of social work at Western Nevada College, clinical director of the Eastern Sierra CISM Team, and cofounder of PsychEd Concepts, Inc. Since 1994, Frank has been a clinical coordinator for Enki Health and Research Systems where he developed a mental health program for a California Distinguished School.

L.A. Watson has been an early-learning education director, multiple subject teacher, special educator, special education administrator, and resource specialist. She has taught in both rural communities and inner-city schools. Lynn is a member of the Eastern Sierra CISM team and cofounder of PsychEd Concepts, Inc.

Photo by Katrina Allmett.

Foreword

Let me be the first to welcome you to this fine book.

I first met Frank Jacobelli at a seminar on bipolar disorder that I was presenting in Sacramento. My presentation included a segment on the 'Executive functions' of the brain, and how the brain can be 'exercised' to improve the functioning of the frontal lobes, thereby improving a person's ability to anticipate consequences, manage impulses, correctly interpret the nonverbal cues of others, and above all, to see one's self 'situationally.' During the seminar, I mentioned that kids, in particular, were very much in need of an activity book that they could use to exercise their frontal lobes and improve executive functioning.

Frank approached me during the break and asked if I would take a look at an activity book that he and his coauthor, a special educator, had been working on for several months. I did, and I was very pleased with what I saw. Finally, a user-friendly, hands-on activity book was born, packed with exactly the kinds of enjoyable activities that kids could use to learn to see themselves 'situationally!'

Since that initial meeting, the original workbook has grown into much more ... a first-of-its kind, information packed book for parents, counselors, and teachers, looking to help kids manage anger and improve executive function, while drawing on the individual learning styles and preferences of the child.

SmartHelp for Good 'n' Angry Kids, a surefire winner, is likely to become the standard bearer by which other books for teaching kids to recognize, process, and express their feelings are measured.

My personal thanks go out to the authors, as well as my warm wishes to you, the reader. May these pages make a real difference in the life of your child.

Dr Jay

(Jay Carter, Psy. D., FPPR (candidate))

Acknowledgments

A note of thanks to Dr. Jay Carter for believing in this book in its infancy, for his 'tweaking of our thinking,' and for instilling in us the confidence required to see this project through to completion. To Stan Wakefield for his incredible ability to repeatedly bridge the gap between an author's dream and a reality in black and white. Thanks to Al Bertrand, Karen Shield, Ruth Jelley, and everyone at Wiley-Blackwell for their efficiency and understated professionalism. Our thanks to Gopika and everyone at Laserwords for their insightful approach in delivering top-notch editing services. And most importantly, we wish to acknowledge the many kids who were our teachers. Thanks to each of you for demanding we recognize your uniqueness.

CHAPTER ONE

Introducing SmartHelp for Good 'n' Angry Kids

The gem cannot be polished without friction.
— Chinese proverb

I doubt you would expect your child to know Algebra if he's never been taught. Is it reasonable then, to expect your child to know how to manage the often misunderstood emotion of anger without having been taught? We think not.

This book provides an all-new approach for allowing your child (for kids aged 9 to 13) to learn the skills necessary to manage (recognize, process, and appropriately express) anger, without having to rely upon the unhealthy and potentially destructive methods he's learned and relied upon until now. We're fairly confident that this describes your child; otherwise, you'd likely be reading the latest blockbuster instead.

SmartHelp is a one-of-a-kind approach to managing anger for two reasons. First, it calls upon your child's individual learning strengths in mastering the necessary skills for managing anger—skills such as self-soothing, accurately interpreting the actions of others, learning from positive role models, and paying attention to the body's warning signs that anger is brewing. Chapter 7 will acquaint you with the concept of individual learning styles, and how using these to overcome learning and behavioral challenges can make all the necessary difference. Thus the name 'SmartHelp.'

Second, we wholeheartedly buy into what the leading neuroscientists have concluded over the past several years: the human brain can change and adapt with proper exercise. The activities contained in this book are geared toward changing your child's brain for the better, strengthening the prefrontal cortex and making it more accessible when needed. The prefrontal cortex, housed within the frontal lobe of your child's brain, which sits just behind the forehead, is responsible for 'executive functions.' With proper executive function comes the ability to anticipate consequences, control impulses, and see one's self 'situationally.' More about your child's brain on anger, in Chapter 2.

But let's back up and take a few moments to acquaint you with how SmartHelp for Good 'n' Angry Kids came to be. We, the coauthors Frank Jacobelli and Lynn Ann Watson, are a mental health counselor and a special educator, with a combined 40 years of experience in our respective fields, having counseled and taught hundreds of kids. Over a period of several years, we worked in the same sparsely populated community and very often with the same challenging, defiant, reactive, disruptive, and just plain angry kids. Enthusiastically, we went about our individual work, using all of our skills, digging deeply into our bags of tricks for just the right teaching tool or counseling strategy. Often frustrated, we began to question why it was that a particular strategy (say, asking a child where it is in his body that he first feels his anger brewing) could work like a charm with one angry child, while the

---

SmartHelp for Good 'n' Angry Kids. By Frank Jacobelli and Lynn Ann Watson
© 2009 Blackwell Publishing, ISBN 978-0-470-75802-1

same strategy would result in a furrowed brow and open-mouthed stare from a different child.

Many hours of discussion ensued, followed by months of trial and error, and then more discussion. Was it possible that the child who was able to respond to the above intervention with 'First I clench my fists, and then I feel a little sick to my stomach. Pretty soon my face feels like its on fire, and then I just want to start swinging!' is a strong *bodily-kinesthetic* learner (see Chapter 7), while the furrowed-browed child is not? Perhaps the furrowed-browed child happens not to have a great deal of awareness of his body, how it feels and how to use it, but is a strong *visual-spatial* learner. Perhaps an intervention better suited to this child is to ask him to look at simple drawings of faces displaying varying degrees of anger. Perhaps this *visual-spatial* learner can use this strategy to identify what kinds of events in his daily life result in which level of anger. Then perhaps, the helper can work with the child in coming up with specific ideas for managing the anger before it escalates to the next level. 'This face is me when I don't get picked for football at playtime.' (Practice memorizing three things you're good at.) 'This is me when my teacher writes my name on the board.' (Remind myself that I will keep my hands to myself in class tomorrow.) 'Here is me when Tommy takes my pencil.' (Let Tommy know that friends don't take things without asking, and carry an extra pencil just in case.)

Before paying attention to the individual learning strengths of kids, Frank was guilty of the same affliction as most mental health professionals. He believed that he could best get through to kids and adult clients alike, simply by talking at them, enlightening them with his *linguistic* insights, and curing their ills with his *spoken* clinical brilliance.

In hindsight, he was long overdue for an ego check. Could it be that mental health professionals and teachers manage to become educated and gainfully employed because *they* happen to be strong *verbal-linguistic* learners in a society (and an educational system) that tends to value those with strong verbal abilities over those who learn best by other means? And are they then trying to reach kids by using the counseling and teaching methods with which *they themselves* are most comfortable?

Was anyone paying attention to the way kids learn best? In fairness, individual learning styles have received a good deal of attention from teachers, particularly special educators, over the past 15 years or so. Far less attention has been paid by counselors and mental health professionals. Special educators had long ago recognized the need to teach 'special' kids by special means, and Lynn (coauthor of this book), as a special educator, had developed a keen interest in the unique and individual abilities of the special kids she taught. It was soon apparent that, not only did these kids learn *more* from teaching methods that took their individual learning strengths into consideration, but when taught by *learning-style aware methods*, these students learned not only the material presented but they learned about themselves as well. Once equipped with knowing their individual learning strengths and preferences, these students were able to educate others in their lives (i.e. parents, teachers, and bosses) on how they can approach a problem outside the classroom in a way that maximizes the chance of solving it—useful self-knowledge that can benefit a child for a lifetime.

Brought together by our joint efforts to reach the same kids in a small community, we realized that if recognizing and using children's individual learning styles could make it easier for them to successfully learn schoolwork, why wouldn't it also be useful to parents, teachers, and counselors striving to help angry kids learn to recognize, process, and appropriately express feelings? Why should the benefits of recognizing and using the individual learning strengths of a child be limited to the special education classroom?

And where was the learning-style aware *workbook* for kids with anger problems that parents, teachers, and counselors could use with their kids, to teach them about anger and what to do with it? Well, it was nowhere to be found, so we came up with this one. And we are very pleased to know that you have it before you at this very moment. First and foremost, SmartHelp for Good 'n' Angry Kids is a compilation of nearly every activity or intervention we have used in our work, to reach and teach the angry child, and arranged according to learning style.

In Appendix 1 you will find the learning style survey and scoring materials; everything you and your child will need to learn about your child's individual learning strengths and interests. The SmartHelp workbook activities (the real 'meat' of this book) are grouped together by learning style. Though simple to use, you will find more detail on how to make the most of the SmartHelp activities with your kids in Chapter 9, titled 'Before You Begin.'

Originally designed simply as a one-of-a-kind workbook, SmartHelp for Good 'n' Angry Kids has evolved into much more. In Chapter 2, we will explore the often ignored, often misunderstood subject of anger. The reader will likely be surprised to learn that even the experts don't agree on a number of the key concepts that surround the topic of anger, and surprisingly, in a world understandably concerned about violent crime, gang violence, schoolyard bullying, school shootings, road rage, and the ravages of war, little research on anger has been scientifically documented.

Is anger a normal, healthy emotion or a human shortcoming? Are some children born angry or do they learn destructive anger from others? How do anger, hostility, and aggression differ? Is it best to simply ignore the things that can make us angry or is this 'stuffing' anger, and is stuffing dangerous to our health, well-being, and relationships?

You will also find an easy-to-understand overview of *your child's brain on anger* in Chapter 2, written by nonscientists for nonscientists.

In Chapter 4 we take a hard look at character. What is it? Is there a character gene or is character taught? If character doesn't come 'factory-installed,' how do we go about instilling it in our kids?

Chapter 5 takes on the uncomfortable topic of 'labeling' children. What determines whether a child is diagnosable or just feisty, high-spirited, or passionate? What are the facts about oppositional defiant disorder (ODD), conduct disorder, and attention deficit disorder (ADD)/attention deficit/hyperactivity disorder (ADHD), and what can be done about the 'symptoms' that result in these unflattering labels being handed out to children?

In Chapter 6 you will learn about getting through to your child, as well as how to create a suitable interpersonal environment for engaging your child in the SmartHelp activities. Additionally, here you will find important strategies for combating the stress that comes with dealing with an angry child—emotional first aid for yourself, if you will.

We will introduce you to a few of the children we have worked with over the years in Chapter 8. You will learn about specific problems and how they were addressed. Most importantly, we will share what we learned from each of the children we discuss. The names of the children, and in some cases, certain specific details that might make the child identifiable, were changed to protect their privacy.

In Chapter 9 you will find important information for making the most of the SmartHelp activities. Included are brief vignettes, geared toward helping you, the 'helper,' parent, teacher, or counselor, get a feel for using a particular SmartHelp activity for addressing certain anger issues or behavior problems. You will be encouraged to develop the theme of each SmartHelp activity with your child, tailoring it to his specific needs. The simple and fun activity can provide a positive framework for healthy quality time for you and your child, crucial for your child's future ability to foster healthy adult relationships.

When working with children having difficulty managing their anger, we have found these SmartHelp activities invaluable for teaching children to better understand their emotions, to self-soothe when necessary, and to see the 'Big Picture' in their interactions with others. A child able to see the big picture is a child less likely to misinterpret the actions of others, better able to put his feelings into context, and more likely to analyze a situation before reacting inappropriately. We are confident that you will have similar results with your kids.

Preserving the anonymity and respecting the confidentiality of our clients, students, and families is the cornerstone of our professional ethics, and of utmost importance. Therefore, names, descriptions, and facts that might make it possible to identify our clients, students, and families, have been altered throughout the text. In some cases, we have blended pertinent facts related to more than one child or family, in an effort to allow the reader to get the most out of the concept we are seeking to convey. None of the case studies discussed is meant to be a complete or completely factual account of any particular child or family's history or progress under our care. In most instances, the facts of the case studies are recounted to the best of our recollection. To make the text more readable, we have often used the pronoun 'he' rather than including both 'he' and 'she.'

We wish you great success in teaching your kids to manage their anger. To grow to be a healthy, happy, and well-adjusted individual is your child's birthright. We are proud you've chosen to bring SmartHelp for Good 'n' Angry Kids along on this very important journey.

◀ CHAPTER TWO ▶

Making Sense of Anger

Passion, though a bad regulator, is a powerful spring.
— Ralph Waldo Emerson, American poet (1803–1882)

Remarkably, little research exists on the topic of anger. In contrast, there is an abundance of books and programs for helping in the management of anger *problems*. Although the majority of these books and programs are geared toward managing anger in adults, we contend that the time to learn about anger is in the beginning, before bad habits become entrenched, and before young brains are wired to respond to anger inappropriately or even destructively. Perhaps, if it were possible, an even more effective approach to behavior management would be to bring children into a world in which aggression is not considered a worthwhile, often acceptable, and at times, even preferred problem-solving strategy. In the words of William Inge, the mid-twentieth-century American playwright, 'The proper time to influence the character of a child is about a hundred years before he's born.'

The authors of the aforementioned books and programs often disagree on some of the core concepts surrounding anger and what to do with it. Is anger a normal human emotion or is it a human shortcoming? Does it serve a worthwhile purpose, needing to be recognized and expressed, or should the goal of the enlightened individual be to rise above the primitive inclination to feel anger in the first place? Are anger and hostility one and the same? Do anger and aggression go hand in hand, or should a distinction be made between anger that is controlled and that which is uncontrolled? Are *bad* people more prone to experience anger than *good* people?

What are your thoughts about anger? Perhaps you haven't given the topic much consideration at all ... until now. The purpose of this chapter is to give you, the parent, teacher, or counselor of an angry child, the opportunity to do just that. Before giving our conclusions to the questions posed earlier, let's give the topic some historical perspective and explore what some of the experts have to say on the subject.

The ancient Greek philosophers, Galen and Seneca, considered anger a type of madness—worthless, even for war, and that 'red-faced people are hot tempered because of excessive hot and dry humors' (Kemp and Strongman, 1995). Aristotle had a slightly different perspective, more in line with modern times, believing that anger had its value, particularly for addressing injustice.

Medieval Christianity rejected anger as one of the seven cardinal, or deadly, sins. Saint Basil regarded it as a 'reprehensible temporary madness' (Fiero), but like Aristotle long before, some Christian writers of the day attributed some value to anger when aroused by injustice.

Early modern philosophers Immanuel Kant and David Hume offered historically relevant views on anger. Kant considered vengeance as vicious—going beyond the defense of man's dignity, while at the same time viewing a lack of responsiveness to social injustice as a sign

SmartHelp for Good 'n' Angry Kids. By Frank Jacobelli and Lynn Ann Watson
© 2009 Blackwell Publishing, ISBN 978-0-470-75802-1

of a lack of 'manhood.' Hume philosophized that 'anger and hatred are passions inherent in our very frame and constitution, the absence of them is sometimes evidence of weakness and imbecility' (Hughes, 2001).

The father of modern psychology, Sigmund Freud, considered anger to result from unconscious processes, and, in a sense, *directional*; meaning that once experienced, it had to go somewhere. Anger not directed at its source in some way is often directed inward, contributing to feelings of guilt and inferiority and the pathological condition of depression.

Semmelroth and Smith, in *The Anger Habit* (2000), remind us that we were all 2-year-olds at one time, and before we had full command of language, we relied on tantrums and other emotional demonstrations to inform our parents that we were hungry, tired, or uncomfortable. Our attention-getting displays of anger were sufficient to make our parents uncomfortable, and therefore willing to respond to our needs. The authors are quick to add that parents don't respond to their child's pain only to make themselves more comfortable. If that were the only reason, they conclude, the lives of children would be quite short indeed. But the critical point is that early on, we learn to control others by making them uncomfortable. When this leads to getting what we want, an important, if not positive, lesson is learned. We can use anger to control others and get them to meet our needs.

Konrad Lorenz—Austrian physician, Nobel Prize winner, and author of *On Aggression* (1971)—contends that anger is a survival instinct, once as critical to man's survival as the drives to hunt for food or get out of the weather. Still, modern man's anger is dangerous and a threat to the survival of the species because of its spontaneity. He has yet to evolve a ritualized impulse-inhibiting mechanism.

For millions of years, some pretty desirable advantages went to the biggest bully in the group. He was the leader of the pack and was shown great respect as the fiercest warrior. He led the hunt and had his choice of sex partners. Author and national lecturer Izzy Kalman (*Bullies to Buddies*, 2005) suggests that man is most likely genetically programmed for aggression, and in nature, might made right. Before man was 'civilized,' problems were solved and status was established by slugging it out. Kalman contends that before there were law enforcement agencies and criminal courts, aggression as a means of maintaining order was essential for survival of the species. On a practical level, it made a good deal of sense by establishing a pecking order. Slugging it out allowed for assessing one's strength in relation to others. The weaker would quickly learn to show respect to the stronger, and in return would be protected. The strength of the stronger became the strength of the weaker, adding to the overall strength and survival of the group.

Kalman further contends that only about 12 000 years ago, when the earth's total population was only about 5 to 10 million (in comparison to about 6 billion today), did our ancestors move away from hunting and gathering and began farming, and it was then that man's instinctual aggression began to lose its value. No longer did man need to compete for the most bountiful hunting ground, and by establishing a home territory, he would less frequently cross the path of his rivals. Though initially primitive, justice systems were established to keep order and provide a rational, nonviolent means for individuals to settle disputes and for societies to defend themselves from wrongdoers.

It may be reasonable to conclude that if man is genetically programmed for anger and aggression as a means of survival over millions of years of evolution, it may not be realistic to assume that he can simply choose to ignore the impulse after only 12 000 years of evolving within a civilized society. While the American Psychological Association concludes that aggression is a learned behavior, Kalman believes it to be instinctual and that anger *management*, and not anger, is a learned behavior.

In contrast to Lorenz and Kalman, McKay, Rogers, and McKay (2003) recount the work of anthropologist Richard Leakey. Leakey concluded that the forms of aggression displayed in the precivilized world were in fact, 'an exercise in competitive display,' as opposed to physical violence, and that 'a species which settles its disputes through violence will reduce its overall fitness and is less likely to survive in an environment that is difficult enough already.' McKay and colleagues go on to summarize, 'it is scientifically incorrect to say that humans have a "violent brain." While we do have the neural apparatus to act violently, there is nothing in our neurophysiology that compels us to do so.'

It's safe to say, the jury is out.

Darcy Sims, clinical psychologist and author of *The Other Side of Grief* (2003), believes that anger begins with grief. She reminds us that anger management is only symptom control, and that intense, disruptive anger in children is most often about unresolved grief, and just the tip of the iceberg. Lacking in the vocabulary to express their hurt, these kids act out their feelings by hitting, yelling, breaking rules, and in other ways 'misbehaving' in order to draw attention to their pain. Unresolved grief fueling intense anger doesn't only result from obviously traumatic tragedies such as physical or sexual abuse, divorce or the incarceration of a parent, but it may also result from less obvious stressors that result from change in a child's life: moving to a new school or neighborhood, a new brother or sister, death of a grandparent or great grandparent, parents fighting, or loss of a pet.

Sims explains the child's grief as resulting from missing the space he used to occupy, or missing the person or object that was occupied by someone or something else. The grief can only be resolved when the child can come to terms with the loss, or can figure out how to fill the space once occupied by another, as in the case of divorce or death.

As a 'helper,' whether a parent, teacher, or counselor, being aware of our child's anger is far from enough. We need to look for and ask about the *hurt*. In some cases, a specially trained child therapist will be needed for helping the angry child uncover the hurt and begin to heal.

▶ Let it Out or Rise Above it?

So then, let's move on to whether the goal should be to recognize and express anger appropriately, or to rise above the inclination to experience the emotion at all.

Mitchell Messer, founder of the Anger Clinic in Chicago and author of *Managing Anger: Handbook of Proven Techniques* (2001), refers to anger as 'the necessary precursor to violence,' the emotion that can blow up a planet, but that no one talks about because it isn't nice. Even trained therapists and counselors often feel unprepared to cope with anger problems in their clients because there is no course in 'Angerology 101' offered in the institutions that prepare counselors to do their work. Messer writes that despite what you've been taught, nice people get angry all the time, but they have learned to 'manage it between the extremes of too much (erupting like a volcano) and too little (smiling through the tears).' While anger is a normal emotion, common to every person on the planet, it is too often expressed destructively. Life gives us an anger problem every 12 minutes, and we are inadequately prepared to solve it.

Messer believes that one of our anger management tools is the power of choice, but 'people keep making the same mistakes because no one ever told them what their other options are.' We often learn about anger as kids, navigating through our early years as part of a family unit. Messer gives the example of the child whose older brother has perfected the art of throwing *tantrums*. Unable to compete, he learns to give *the silent treatment* and hones the technique to a fine art, thereby drawing a clear contrast between his brother's personality and his own. In another family, unable to compete with the *screaming* of a baby sister, her bigger brother may opt for *sarcasm*, and this unproductive anger management technique can last a lifetime. Messer concludes that 'we learn anger management in the same way' that we learn to wash dishes or make beds . . . in the area of anger management, there hasn't been a brain cell working for four generations.'

Contrary to Messer and others who consider anger to be a normal part of the human condition, there are those who believe that the goal of anger management should be to avoid experiencing this destructive emotion in the first place.

Between March 2000 and fall of 2001, a unique dialog took place in the quarters of the Dalai Lama in Dharamsala, India, between leaders in two disciplines generally not thought of as sharing a similar train of thought. The Buddhist spiritual leader and a small group of renowned scientists and philosophers engaged in a discussion of *destructive emotions*. The result is a book by the same name (2003) and it makes for fascinating reading. Buddhism considers what Western psychology refers to as 'emotion' as destructive, obstructing mental clarity and emotional equilibrium, and therefore needing to be overcome. The Dalai Lama lists the three destructive states known in Buddhism as the Three Poisons: anger, craving, and delusion.

In an exchange between the Dalai Lama and Dr Paul Ekman, professor of psychology at the University of California at San Francisco Medical School, Ekman states that, though he has no proof, he believes that anger response is a built-in mechanism designed to remove an obstacle that's thwarting us, but that this response or impulse doesn't always require violence. The Dalai Lama counters, commenting on the Buddhist belief that tolerance and anger are opposites, and that tolerance or patience in the face of harm caused by others is the opposite of violence. The Dalai Lama is quick to acknowledge the difficulty he finds in separating anger and violence. The spiritual leader doggedly contends that anger is 'afflictive' or destructive, and the goal of the enlightened mind should be to overcome whatever innate tendency we may have to experience it.

In a similar vein, psychologist and national lecturer Lynn Johnson suggests that we begin to view anger as one of many habits we've grabbed on to over time, some good and some bad. Anger, he suggests, interferes with our ability to find happiness and satisfaction in our lives, and is generally not helpful. In *Get on the Peace Train* (2004), Johnson writes that anger doesn't help 'unless your aim is to destroy your opponent,' and this destructive emotion likely serves us well in battle. But off the battlefield, anger is counterproductive, making us more rigid, less intelligent, and less capable of healthy relationships. Johnson goes on to say that anger creates more problems than it solves, and 'is a classic case of the cure for a problem being worse than the disease.'

▶ Your Child's Brain on Anger

To teach your child to process and express anger differently is to teach him to use his brain differently.

Never before in history has the scientific community given so much attention to the human brain, and the findings are astounding. Perhaps the most important discovery in recent years is that the brain can physically change and adapt, possibly throughout a lifetime. This ability to change as a result of experience is a concept scientists refer to as neuroplasticity or just 'plasticity.' If the brain were not 'plastic,' meaning capable of adapting through experience or 'exercise,' there would be no reason for this book.

Practitioners ourselves, we don't claim to be scientists or experts on the brain, but we have learned from those who are on the cutting edge of neurobiology—scientists such as Joseph Ledoux, Elkhonon Goldberg, Daniel Amen, Daniel Siegel, Louis Cozolino, Daniel Goleman, and Bruce Perry. Many of the works by these fine researchers are understandable and enjoyable to read by nonscientists like us (and most likely you) and we highly recommend them to those interested in learning about the brain and how it works. The titles are listed in the reference section at the back of this book.

In the interest of getting the most out of this book for you and your child, a brief overview of *your child's brain on anger* is in order. We recognize the simplistic nature of the explanation to follow, and we apologize in advance to any neuroscientists who may be among the readers of this book.

That which your child perceives from the outside world (external stimuli) is delivered to the *thalamus*, a structure that sits at the top of the brain's stem, deep in the 'reptilian' part of the brain (see Figure 2.1). A 'motherboard' of sorts, the thalamus passes on these signals in two directions and at different speeds: to the *amygdala* (the down and dirty low road), and to the *neocortex*, an outermost structure (located in the frontal lobes) responsible for reasoning. The amygdala's job is to make a quick determination as to any threat that might be contained in those incoming signals, and to tell your child to respond immediately if it's determined that the stimulus is a danger. An example of this low road being a necessary survival mechanism is, if your child were to place his hand on a hot stove. Taking the time to think about what the consequences might be (Hey, I could get burned doing something like this. Maybe I should consider taking my hand off the stove!) is the kind of response that doesn't support the survival of a species. The low road allows for a super-quick (fight or flight), nonthinking response to a threat.

Because there are more connections involved, the signal that the thalamus relays to the neocortex is about a quarter second behind the signal to the amygdala. But once the signal does pass through the neocortex, the information delivered to the amygdala is much more complete (the high road). This additional information is likely to provide the person with the 'big picture' and therefore lead to a more productive, thought-out, and nonreactive response. This is the reason for the popularity of the often recommended 'count to 10' approach for managing anger, and Swindoll's '3-second pause,' discussed in Chapter 4.

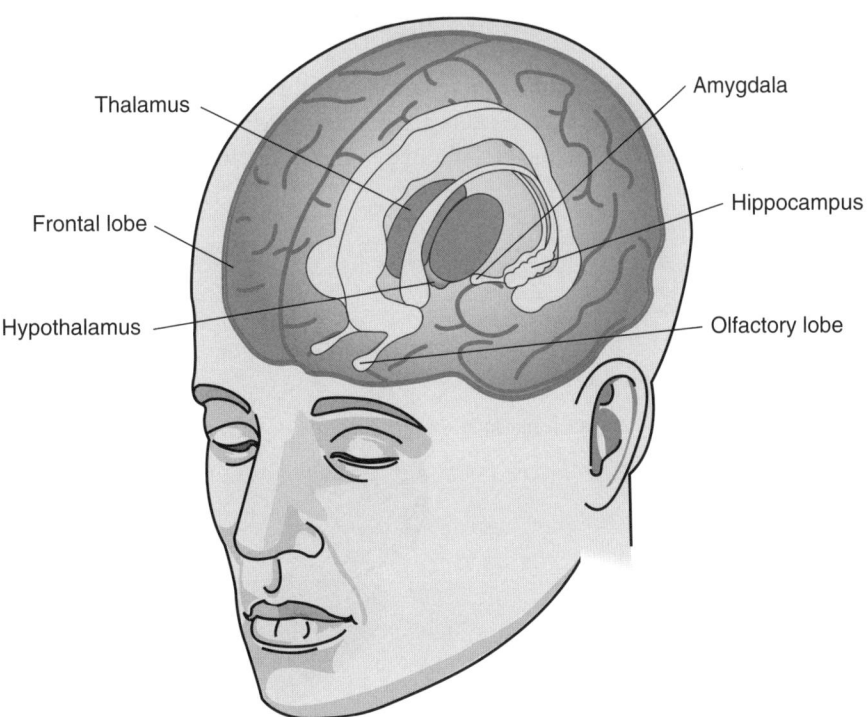

Figure 2.1 The Limbic System and Frontal Lobe

▶ The 'High Road' in Managing Anger

The high road involves both the reptilian part of the brain and the neocortex, a part of the brain's frontal lobe (see Figure 2.2). Maybe you've noticed that you tend to be a bit more irritable if you haven't eaten in a while. That's just the kind of information that you would store in your neocortex. Now, let's say that your spouse is late in meeting you at your favorite restaurant for your regularly scheduled Thursday night date. There you sit, stomach rumbling, the aroma of your favorite dish in the air, and your cell phone begins to ring. Your wife is calling to tell you that your date completely slipped her mind and even if she left work at that very moment, she wouldn't arrive at the restaurant for nearly an hour.

A reaction resulting strictly from the *low road* processing of your wife's news (ear to thalamus to amygdala, and bypassing the neocortex before your response) just might result in a few choice words that could put you in the dog house. Whereas, delaying your response so that you can use the reasoning abilities of your neocortex is likely to lead to a far more favorable consequence. (I know how short-tempered I can be when I'm hungry. Let's not overreact. Sally's had a lot on her mind lately, between the kids and her job. Might be best to take a couple of deep breaths before I open my mouth.) A well-developed and accessible neocortex might even result in some 'super-planning' to solve the immediate problem at hand. Perhaps you will offer to bring dinner home to the family, order the takeout, and have an appetizer while you're waiting.

In *Destructive Emotions*, Dr Mark Greenberg, professor of human development at Pennsylvania State University, writes that first learning is easiest, and that later learning is more difficult because it's *relearning*. The right lessons at the right age interplay with the development of the brain. The best time for lessons on emotional regulation is during early and mid-childhood, when the brain structures involved—the prefrontal areas, the amygdala, and the hippocampus—are truly coming online.

Because the brain is 'plastic,' particularly in young children, early childhood experiences are crucial in determining how the brain will ultimately function throughout a lifetime. Nurturing experiences, such as those contained in the workbook activities, are akin to *health food* for the neocortex, the part of the brain responsible for reasoning and impulse control. Our firm belief, based on over 40 years of combined experience teaching and counseling kids, is that the *high road* can be cultivated and made more accessible to kids, with practice. And when the lessons are presented with consideration for how the individual child learns best, as are those contained in this book, the results can be remarkable.

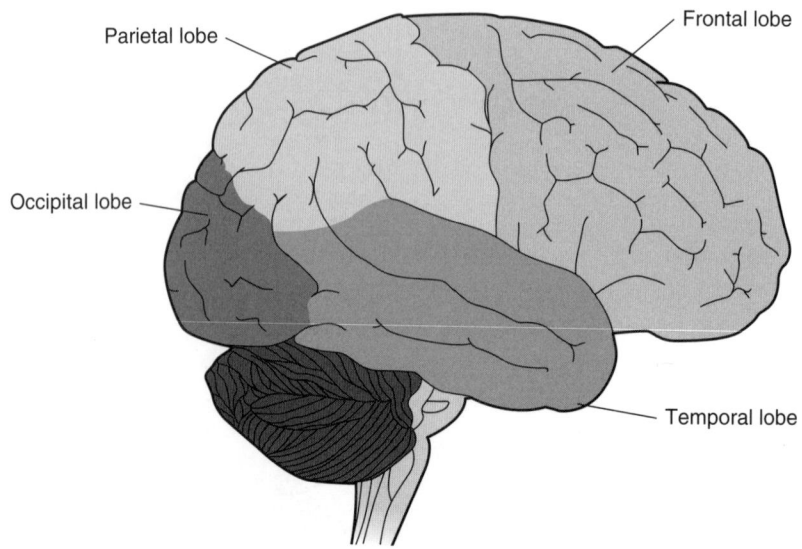

Figure 2.2 The Lobes of the Brain

Until recently, the medical profession has been reluctant to accept a direct relationship between brain function and behavior. This has been particularly frustrating for Dr Daniel Amen, a clinical neuroscientist, psychiatrist, medical director of the Amen Clinic in Fairfield, California, and author of *Change Your Brain, Change Your Life* (1999). Dr Amen uses single photon emission computed tomography (SPECT), a kind of brain scan that measures cerebral blood flow and metabolic activity patterns to study the brains of patients with learning, emotional, or behavior problems that haven't responded to the treatments normally prescribed for such individuals. After studying over 30 000 SPECT scans, Amen has made a strong case for a brain–behavior connection, and the scientific community has begun to listen.

One such patient was Andrew, a 9-year-old, whom Amen identifies as his godson and nephew. Previously a happy and active child, Andrew had begun having homicidal and suicidal thoughts, and angry outbursts that culminated in Andrew attacking a little girl on the baseball field. A SPECT scan performed by Amen revealed a large cyst in the area of the left temporal lobe of Andrew's brain. The cyst was so large that the temporal lobe appeared nearly nonexistent on the scan. The left temporal lobe has long been an area of the brain associated with anger.

Amazingly, because of a long-standing resistance by the medical profession to link brain and behavior, Dr Amen had difficulty convincing any surgeon to operate on Andrew. Several had indicated that they would do so only when some 'real symptoms' (p. 13), such as seizures or speech problems, appeared. Infuriated, Amen persisted until a neurosurgeon took Andrew's case, and the surgery was a complete success. After removal of the large cyst, Andrew was once again the happy, playful child he had previously been—further evidence that there is indeed a link between the functioning of the brain and behavior.

We will touch on the Amen Clinic again in Chapter 8, when we tell you about Thomas, one of our most memorable kids. We were fortunate enough to, while attending a lecture by Dr Amen and on break, offer our thanks for his pioneering efforts, and for trying to help Thomas.

▶ Phineas and the Frontal Lobe

The tragic case of Phineas Gage, a railroad construction foreman who suffered a tragic accident in 1848, is well-documented evidence that the frontal lobes of the brain have direct bearing on personality and a person's ability to interact appropriately with others. While blasting rock, Gage filled a drilled hole with gun powder and began using a tamping iron to compact the powder at the bottom of the hole. Momentarily distracted, Gage wasn't aware that his coworker had not yet added the sand to the hole that was to act as a buffer to prevent sparking. The gun powder was ignited prematurely and the 3-foot-long tamping iron, 1.25 inches in diameter and weighing over 13 pounds, was launched with such force that it passed through Gage's skull and landed almost 100 feet away. The rod entered his skull below the left cheek bone, passed through the anterior frontal cortex and exited at the top of Gage's skull. Remarkably, Gage regained consciousness within a few minutes.

Phineas Gage returned to his job 6 months after the accident but his personality had radically changed. While Gage was previously hard-working, responsible, and popular with his men, the injury to the frontal lobes of his brain left him impatient, fitful, irreverent, impulsive, and prone to using gross profanity. Soon fired from his job and unable to maintain steady employment, Gage spent a year as a sideshow attraction, alongside the rod that caused his injury, with the PT Barnum New York Museum. He later drove a coach in South America, and eventually returned to San Francisco where he lived with his mother. In 1860, Gage began to experience epileptic seizures and died a few months later.

The misfortune of Phineas Gage provided the scientific community with early evidence that brain health and brain function, particularly the functioning of the frontal lobe, have a direct bearing on a person's behavior. Still, it would be another 100 years or so until the necessary technology would make it possible to just begin to understand the nature of the brain–behavior connection. Even in the early part of the twenty-first century, true understanding is only in its infancy.

▶ Kids and Trauma

According to Dr Bruce Perry—neuroscientist, child psychiatrist, and internationally recognized authority on childhood trauma—children exposed to trauma and neglect in childhood, especially those receiving a steady dose, are likely to have brains that are in a constant state of 'fear activation.' The traumatized child, as a means of survival, is forced to view the world as a place to fear, where danger is looming and life-threatening violence may erupt at any moment. Because the brain is 'use dependent,' a traumatized child's brain becomes organized in a manner that results in the child being in a constant state of hypervigilance, increased muscle tone, and focusing on fear-related cues—in other words, a child feeling constant fear and always ready to fight or flee. Perry writes, 'This is the dilemma that traumatic abuse brings to the child's developing brain. The very process of using the proper adaptive neural response during a threat will also be the process that underlies the neural pathology, which causes so much pain through the child's life' (The Impact of Abuse and Neglect on the Developing Brain, p.1).

Perry, both neuroscientist and child psychiatrist, has the rare perspective necessary to investigate across disciplines—exploring both the psychological and biological consequences of violence in the lives of kids. Among his findings is that a child's brain between birth and age 3 has an amazing ability to absorb information and experiences, for example, to become fluent in a language, simply by being in the proximity of caregivers speaking that language. This same ability to efficiently absorb *brain-changing* life experiences is responsible for the young child's brain absorbing chaos, violence, and the damaging effects of neglect and abuse when exposed to these *negative* brain-changing life experiences. The biological results often include a significantly smaller amygdala and corpus callosum, a poorly organized prefrontal cortex, and a temporal lobe with a greater chance of causing temporal lobe epilepsy, than in kids who are nurtured, protected, and not regularly exposed to violence. Perry has clearly demonstrated that neglect and exposure to violence can negatively impact brain development.

More on the effects of trauma and violence on children is given in Chapter 5.

▶ Authors' Take on Anger

We wish to begin by encouraging the reader intending to teach a child about feelings to think in terms of only five feeling states, *angry* being one. The others are *happy*, *sad*, *scared*, and *confused*. The easier we can make it for kids to identify a feeling, the more likely they will be to call upon the appropriate manner of expressing that feeling. We are familiar with the popular feelings posters, puzzles, and workbooks that contain as many as 100 feelings. How confusing this must be to a child who can barely distinguish his/her anger from sadness!

We contend that one can list the five feeling states (happy, sad, angry, scared, and confused) across the top of a blackboard, and beneath each, list as many as 10 or 15 'feelings' that have pretty much the same meaning. Rather than overwhelm a young prefrontal cortex with 100 feeling words and asking the attached child to distinguish among them, we've found it to be much more efficient to teach that we sometimes feel more than one feeling at a time, and to different degrees. For example, what is *disappointed* if not a mixture of sad and angry? Isn't irritated the same as a *little* angry? Do we really want to give kids the message that it's necessary to distinguish between confused and *perplexed*? Sad and *sorrowful*? Very angry and *enraged*? We acknowledge that using colorful, highly descriptive words to describe feelings can be fun and can add another dimension to a lively discussion, but let's start kids off with the basics. There will be plenty of time for them to learn flamboyant language later, when their brains are more fully developed.

Now, as for what to do with anger specifically, imagine an empty teacup sitting on a tabletop in front of you. Now imagine that each time something angers (irritates, annoys, frustrates, etc.) you, a *small* pebble is dropped into the cup. (If you are abused, neglected, or are exposed to other serious trauma or loss, a large and potentially damaging *stone*.) What might happen as these pebbles continue to accumulate? When your cup is full, what will happen when more pebbles are added?

The anger response to a cup running over is about frustration born of a lack of control. 'I can't fix it!' flies in the face of the always hopeful human spirit.

We contend that taking pebbles into our cup is a normal part of life. Some pebbles are larger than others, and they sometimes land with a lot of force. But regardless of their size or velocity, our cup will continue to fill unless we have a way of keeping our cup from filling with pebbles. To keep our cup clean, we need to be able to recognize and process hurt and anger as we experience it, that is, each time a pebble is added to our cup. Once we've become aware of our hurt and/or anger (the presence of a pebble), we need tools for tossing the pebbles from our cup, that is, to express our anger and come to terms with our hurt in appropriate ways. By keeping our cup clean, we never have to experience the overwhelming and miserable condition of a cup overflowing with pebbles, and putting us at risk of acting out anger destructively.

Perhaps the civil rights movement was begun by an African-American woman who had become all too aware of the accumulation of pebbles in her cup, and decided it was time for a good cleaning, refusing to give her seat on the bus to a white man. Perhaps some angry colonists, sensing their cups would soon overflow with pebbles, decided upon founding a new nation, as a productive means of 'cup hygiene.' Let us not forget that anger, when expressed appropriately, can be personally energizing, and even essential to positive societal change.

While we may be wired to naturally respond to a perceived threat with aggression, violence and other forms of destructive behavior are too often the result of lacking alternative means of responding to anger when it's experienced. While anger may often be a precursor to aggression, aggression does not always have to follow anger.

Who can deny that for most of the time that man has been around, he lived in a wild, uncivilized world? In the wild, man relied on his ability to respond to threat without delay in order to survive. That response often required aggression as well as the emotion that often came before it. Anger in the precivilized era may have served man well. As man's brain evolved, however, and his frontal cortex grew, he began to rely on alternative ways to deal with situations and people who were perceived as threatening, and ultimately, a justice system was created. Man could begin to use his big brain to reason and analyze the 'threat' and place it in context. Not every slight or insult was a threat to his survival, and so it might not be necessary to respond with aggression. There had to be other ways to solve conflict. The sifting through of alternative ways of dealing with conflict continues to this day.

We find ourselves in the fortunate circumstance of having a brain like no other creature on earth: one with a highly evolved frontal cortex, giving us the unique ability to analyze, reason, plan, anticipate consequences, and see ourselves 'situationally.' But like having a computer and no operating system, the hardware can only be fully operational when loaded with *task-specific* software. Anger management software for the young frontal cortex can be found in this book, in the workbook activities.

The ability to acknowledge, process, and respond to anger without aggression and destructive behavior can improve with practice, and many of our kids haven't had the practice they need. Young brains that haven't practiced effective anger-management skills will rely on whatever means they may have at hand to respond to the crashing of pebbles inside their cups, or to a perceived threat. The kids we've taught and counseled have had remarkable success in substituting the useful skills contained in this book for the destructive ones they relied on previously.

While the authors respect and admire those who believe that anger should be avoided and never experienced, and consider this a superb and worthwhile goal, we doubt this can be accomplished by many of us within the course of our life spans. Perhaps it will first be necessary for mankind to continue to evolve for quite some time. Still, it's somehow comforting to know that there are those among us, such as the Tibetan spiritual leaders, who hold true to this ideal.

◀ CHAPTER THREE ▶

Major Theories about Anger: A Brief, Annotated Guide

We state in Chapter 2 that there are few scientific studies on anger. Perhaps this is due in part to the ambiguity of the term itself, or its multidimensional nature. Is anger observable? Or is it purely an emotional state, only observable when it has successfully fueled something else, for example, hostility, and a physical act of aggression? There are plenty of studies on aggression.

But perhaps unobservable anger can be observed after all, say, by measuring some of its physiological effects—heart rate, blood pressure, and blood vessel constriction. But then is it still anger that is being studied, or is it stress, the adrenocortical physiology that comes from hyperarousal, or something else?

Recognizing the ambiguity of the term in many people's minds and anger's multidimensional nature, we nonetheless find value in the philosophical and sometimes scientific theories put forth by leaders in the field. We've therefore included a brief, historical annotated guide to the theories of anger here, for the reader interested in further study and consideration of the topic. We've included only a handful of theories and suggested readings. Omissions do not represent a lack of respect for other theories or theorists, but rather a commitment to brevity.

Anger: A feeling of displeasure resulting from injury, mistreatment, opposition, usually showing itself in a desire to fight back at the supposed cause of this feeling (*Webster's New World Dictionary* 1988).

Anger has some value, particularly when in response to social injustice. The opposite of anger is a kind of senselessness. The differences among people's temperaments are the result of the different mixes of humors within the individual human body (Aristotle. Ancient Greek philosopher, c. 384 BC–322 BC).

Suggested readings:

Aristotle. *The Nicomachean Ethics* (Penguin classics), 2003.
Complete Works of Aristotle, Volume 2 (Princeton University Press), 1984.

Anger is a result of excessive hot and dry humors, is a kind of madness, and even suicide is preferable to rage. Anger is considered 'worthless, even for war' (Seneca. Ancient Greek philosopher, c. 4 BC–AD 65).

Suggested reading:

Kemp, S., Strongman, K. Anger theory and management: A historical analysis. *The American Journal of Psychology*, **108**(3), 1995.

SmartHelp for Good 'n' Angry Kids. By Frank Jacobelli and Lynn Ann Watson
© 2009 Blackwell Publishing, ISBN 978-0-470-75802-1

Anger is the desire for vengeance. Reasonable vengeance and passion is not only acceptable, but praiseworthy. Vengeance is only wrong when excessive and when it becomes opposed to justice and charity, or is targeted upon someone who doesn't deserve it (Delany, J. Contributor to the *Catholic Encyclopedia*, 1914.)

'Turn the other cheek.' Violence should not be a reaction to aggression (Jesus Christ, from the Sermon on the Mount. The New Testament of the Bible. Matthew 5: 38–42).

Anger is one of three powers possessed in the hearts of animals; the other two being appetite and impulse, and *animal* will is conditioned by anger and appetite. *Human* will, on the other hand, is conditioned by *intellect* (Al-Ghazali. Medieval Persian philosopher, 1058–1111).

Suggested reading:

Haque, A. Psychology from Islamic perspective: Contributions of early Muslim scholars and challenges to contemporary Muslim psychologists. *Journal of Religion and Health*, **43**(4), [367] 2004.

Anger is an inherent component of the human makeup. When anger and hatred are lacking, this may be evidence of weakness and imbecility (David Hume. Scottish philosopher, 1711–1776).

Suggested reading:

Hughes, P. *'Anger'*. *Encyclopedia of Ethics*, Volume 1, Second Edition, 2001.

Aggression is innate to the human personality, and often results from psychological trauma or unconscious conflict. Unless the person is made conscious of the trauma or conflict and is able to express the feelings appropriately, one's anger might be turned on the self, resulting in feelings of guilt, inferiority, and depression (Sigmund Freud. Austrian neurologist and founder of psychoanalysis, 1856–1939).

Suggested readings:

Freud, S. *A General Introduction to Psychoanalyisis* (Pocket Books), 1952.
New Introductory Lectures on Psychoanalysis (W.W. Norton), 1965.
The Psychopathology of Everyday Life (Mentor), 1958.
The Interpretation of Dreams (Modern Library), 1995.

Aggression is one of the four basic drives instinctual to all humans (the others being hunger, sex, and fear). Man has not yet evolved any ritualized aggression-inhibiting mechanism, putting the survival of the species at risk. Anger is dangerous because of its spontaneity and potential for causing harm. Modern humans are 'in transition,' too prideful and arrogant to learn from the behavior of animals, but moving toward becoming higher beings or 'real humans' (Konrad Lorenz 2002).

Suggested readings:

Lorenz, K. *On Aggression* (Rutledge Classics), 2002.
Behind the Mirror: A Search for a Natural History of Human Knowledge (Harvest Books), 1978.

Anger may serve as an effective manipulation strategy, particularly when feigned or exaggerated, for achieving goals and influencing society.

Suggested readings:

Sutton, R. 'Maintaining norms about expressed emotions: The case of bill collectors'. *Administrative Services Quarterly*, 1991.

Hochschild, A. *The Managed Heart: Commercialization of Human Feeling* (University of California Press), 1983.
Semmelroth, C. and Smith, D. *The Anger Habit*, 2000.

Anger is a destructive 'emotional affliction' resulting from emotional bias or a distorted view. Anger can be counteracted by cultivating loving kindness. This is done by attending to certain facets of reality that arouse compassion and loving kindness. Buddhist philosophy draws a distinction between anger aroused by biased perception, and clear, forceful action against evil, and offers a model for mobilizing moral outrage in the service of compassion (Buddhist philosophy).

Suggested readings:

Dalai Lama and Goldman, D. *Destructive Emotions*, 2003.
Johnson, L. *Get on the Peace Train: A Journey from Anger to Harmony*, 2004.

Destructive anger is often the result of unresolved grief, particularly in children, who lack the vocabulary to express their feelings of loss and helplessness.

Suggested readings:

Sims, D. and Franklin, A. *The Other Side of Grief*, 2003.
Webb, N. *Helping Bereaved Children*, Second Edition, (Guilford Press), 2002.
Perry, B. and Szalavitz, M. *The Boy Who Was Raised by a Dog: And Other Stories from a Child Psychiatrist's Notebook—What Traumatized Children Can Teach Us about Loss, Love, and Healing*, (Basic Books), 2007.

Anger is a survival tool, honed over hundreds of thousands of years during man's pre-civilized period, necessary for defining the social hierarchy. The most feared became the leader, having his choice of hunting grounds and sexual partners. The weaker aligned behind the stronger, and his strengths became their strength, ultimately benefiting the entire clan. Only over the past 12 000 years or so, since man has developed a centralized justice system, has man not depended on anger and aggression as a means of maintaining order. Still, the genetic programming remains.

Suggested readings:

Leakey, R. and Lewin, R. *Origins: The Emergence and Evolution of Our Species and Its Possible Future* (Penguin non-classics), 1991.
Lorenz, K. *On Aggression* (Rutledge classics), 2002.
Kalman, I. *Bullies to Buddies*, 2005.

Early childhood experiences, particularly exposure to violence, may result in a poorly organized brain that is prone to violence. These biological factors, combined with a deteriorating social fabric, focus less on nurturing and protective caregiving, and the false belief that children are 'resilient' and less vulnerable to the emotional impact of trauma than are adults combine to form a framework for understanding the increasing violence in American youth.

Suggested readings:

Perry, B. and Szalavitz, M. *The Boy Who Was Raised by a Dog: And Other Stories from a Child Psychiatrist's Notebook—What Traumatized Children Can Teach Us about Loss, Love, and Healing* (Basic Books), 2007.
Perry, B. 'Safe from the Start' (video). (California Attorney General's Office), 2004.
Cozolino, L. *The Neuroscience of Human Relationships: Attachment and the Developing Social Brain*, 2006.
Amen, D. *Change Your Brain, Change Your Life*, 1998.

◀ CHAPTER FOUR ▶

Character: Factory Installed or Add-On Equipment?

What a man's mind can create, a man's character can control.
— Thomas Edison, American inventor (1847–1931)

In preparing to write a book for parents, teachers, and counselors of angry kids, we couldn't help but visit the subject of character. By including this chapter, we don't mean to imply that kids who have trouble managing their anger are necessarily lacking in character. Still, ignoring the relationship between the inappropriate expression of anger and its relationship to a person's character, we decided, would be a disservice to the reader. While the inappropriate expression of anger in children is most often due to a lack of skills, a well-developed character is essential for respecting one's self and others, and moderating emotions that might otherwise lead to destructive behavior.

While personality might be defined as a set of thought, behavioral, and emotional characteristics that is relatively consistent in a person over time, character and personality are not one and the same. Character is best defined as the internal motivation to do the right thing, even when no one is watching. In *Educating with Character* (1989), developmental psychologist and educator Thomas Lickona writes that character is 'knowing the good, desiring the good, and doing the good.'

But where does a person's character come from? Has science yet identified a 'character gene?' Could inherited character explain why some kids, seemingly exposed only to negative influences, can mange to function with character in a dysfunctional setting? Is a person's character factory installed or is it add-on equipment?

Twin studies have long been the researcher's method of choice in trying to determine the role of genetics vs. environmental factors, on everything from intelligence, to ADHD, to schizophrenia. The fact that identical twins share all of their genes, and fraternal twins share 50% has made the study of twins a valuable tool for researchers trying to solve the nature vs. nurture dilemma for over 100 years. With regard to a person's behavior, some scientific and anecdotal findings have been so astounding as to send a shiver up scientists' spines. A case in point in the twin studies literature is that of Barbara Herbert and Daphne Goodship (*Psychology Today*, 1997). The sisters were introduced to the public via syndicated television talk shows some 20 years ago. Both had been adopted as babies into separate British families after their Finnish mother committed suicide. Once reunited, it was determined that both women left school at age 14, met their future husbands at age 16 at the town hall dance, went to work in local government, miscarried in the same month, and both eventually gave birth to two boys and a girl. Both drank their coffee cold, had tinted their hair auburn, and were wearing cream-colored dresses and brown velvet jackets when they met. With regard to physical similarities aside from those obviously present in their outward appearance, both women had the same heart murmur and thyroid problems. Their IQ test scores were just one point apart.

SmartHelp for Good 'n' Angry Kids. By Frank Jacobelli and Lynn Ann Watson
© 2009 Blackwell Publishing, ISBN 978-0-470-75802-1

Needless to say, during the years following their reunification, the twins were studied for several years by eager scientists, at the University of Minnesota's Center for Twin Adoption Research.

This particular twin observation is so phenomenal as to nearly make one question the notion of free will in shaping one's life, giving credence to the point of view that nature (genetics) plays a far greater role in shaping us and our lives than does nurture. When the totality of twin studies research is taken into account, however, environment and life experiences have been determined to play a role generally equal to that of genetics.

Genetics and environmental influences in aggressive and antisocial behavior have been studied extensively. Genetic predispositions have been shown to play a significant role in adult aggressive behavior, especially with regard to impulsive aggressive behavior (Coccaro et al. 1997).

Sadly, few studies have been specific to kids. But in 2001, University of Southern California psychologists were given a $1.8 million grant from the National Institute of Mental Health to launch a landmark study on human aggression. The research team, led by professor of psychology, Dr Laura Baker, tracked the mentality and behavior of 600 pairs of 9-year-old ethnically diverse twins over their adolescence. The study revealed a common 'ASB factor' (antisocial and aggressive behavior) that was *strongly* heritable, meaning, attributable to genetic variations (Baker et al. 2007). The interested reader should consider reading this study in detail. The reference is included at the end of the book.

Also of interest when evaluating the studies of aggression and antisocial behavior in children is that these behaviors are often in the eye of the beholder. For example, when a study's design calls for raters to observe the kids, such as mother, father, teacher, and the kids themselves, there is very seldom a 'shared view of what constitutes aggressive or antisocial behavior. Typically, 1.00 being total agreement, mother and father ratings correlate at about 0.60, just 0.28 for parent and teacher, and only 0.22 between child and parent' (Achenbach, McConaughty, and Howell 1987). We have found similar differing judgments of children's behavior in our work. Often, a teacher or principal will find a student's behavior totally unacceptable and push for the child to be seen in mental health counseling. But when the parent is contacted and the behavior problems described to the parents, they are of the opinion that 'boys will be boys,' or 'Sally is just sensitive.' Although it is sometimes frustrating to the teacher, a child can only enter mental health counseling with the parent's permission in most cases. If the parent doesn't see a problem, the child is unlikely to receive the services that the school personnel may feel will benefit him. On some occasions, the parents will give permission for the child to enter treatment, more as a means of pacifying the school than out of any true determination that their child is in need of mental health counseling.

In all our years of working with kids and families, we've been consistently fascinated with those kids who, despite horrific family circumstances, exposure to tragic emotional traumas, and desperately lacking in healthy role models, seem somehow to have a kind of internal *golden compass*: some guiding light that allows them to stay on the higher path. To understand these kids is to have a leg up in building character in all kids.

These 'character-equipped' kids are oftentimes chronic worriers: tense and anxious little people who see the dysfunction around them for what it is, and are determined to find their way out, through, or around it. They are oftentimes devoted to making things better for those around them, particularly those people who continue to struggle with bad choices and their consequences. Much of the energy these kids have for 'making it' then, is siphoned off, leaving them with barely enough to cope. The workbook activities in this book, with a helper's assistance, serve double duty as emotional reinforcement for these kids.

In *Building Moral Intelligence* (2001), Michele Borba, educational psychologist and author of 18 books for parents and educators, refers to your child's *moral core* as consisting of empathy, conscience, and self-control. Borba believes that moral intelligence is learned, and is necessary to ward off the negative influences. 'Moral intelligence will be the muscle he needs to counter those negative pressures and will give him the power to act right with or without your influence' (p. 5). She believes that parents are waiting too long, often until the children are 6 or 7, the widely accepted benchmark for the age of reason, to provide necessary moral guidance to their kids.

But if Borba is right and character is learned, how can we explain the character-equipped kids—those who seemingly have been exposed mostly or entirely to negative influences? Are these kids evidence that character is indeed 'factory installed' in some kids?

A model supporting the link between genetics and character is the NPA theory of personality, developed by A.M. Benis, based on the work of psychiatrist Karen Horney. Benis proposes that there are three major behavioral traits underlying personality: narcissism (N), perfectionism (P), and aggression (A), and that each trait is based on a gene that determines several related characteristics, following the rules of Mendelian genetics. The model holds that a person's character type is to a large extent determined by which of these genes is dominant, and which are recessive.

When the A type (aggression) is dominant, Horney believed, a person is prone to 'move against people.' This person is likely to be arrogant and vindictive, and in extreme cases, sadistic and paranoid. According to NPA theory, the Aggressive gene might be subdued, depending on the presence and relative dominance of the Perfectionism and Narcissism genes. Benis concedes that despite being decades old, the NPA model has not been scientifically proven. He adds that the same is true of other personality theories, and with the relatively recent advances in deciphering the human genome, science may someday be able to prove the relationship between genetics and personality.

In the mean time, it is universally accepted that both genetic and environmental factors ('nature and nurture') play a role in the development of personality. And while there may someday be scientific evidence that the genes a person is born with contribute to his character, we are convinced that a person's character is largely determined by the quality of the love he receives as a child.

Perhaps despite being exposed mostly to negative influences, the character-equipped child was also exposed to one or more positive influences—a buffer of sorts, somehow allowing the child to identify alternative ways of thinking and coping. Often, that buffer is one or more adults with something to offer—a parent, teacher, counselor, coach, or a relative who takes a special interest, and considers any energy invested in this child to be a worthwhile investment in his future.

Most often, those kids who manage to develop character in the midst of chaos are those who are aware of some special quality they possess. Be it a talent for math or storytelling, baseball or dance, the particular special quality matters little. But once the special trait is identified for them, and they are allowed to develop it, the child may eventually have the opportunity to give it back to the world in some meaningful way. Whether or not the child is successful in developing and giving back their talent, the knowledge that they are special in some way, and the positive energy expended on practicing and refining that talent, may act as a buffer against poor decisions and will likely be a catalyst for character. We encourage you, the 'helper,' to use the learning style information contained in this book, as a jumping-off point for helping your child to identify and develop their special quality, with an eye toward giving it back to the world. You will be building into your child some protection against apathy, temptation, mediocrity, and despair.

▶ Parenting with Restraint

Clark, Dawson, and Bredehoft, authors of *How Much is Enough?* (2004), studied adults who were 'overindulged' as children. The authors identify three ways of overindulging kids that interfere with character development. The first is *Too Much Giving*. These kids are showered with 'stuff.' They are likely to grow up to be adults who can never have enough—enough money, sex, food, fun—whatever. They may become spendthrifts, workaholics, or thrill-seekers, with a tendency to take things to the extreme. The ability to achieve a healthy balance in life may be a seemingly impossible, lifelong challenge.

The second type of overindulgence is *Overnurturing*. This happens when adults routinely do things for kids that they should be doing for themselves. These kids often grow up to live a life role in which they appear cute, helpless, and manipulative. The overnurtured child will eventually move into adulthood unprepared, and is likely to rely on others to have their basic needs met. Clark and colleagues give the example of a college freshman who is mortified when she finds she is the only one in her dorm who has no clue how to operate a washer and dryer. A more serious example might be the young woman who, fearful of a life in which she will need to start from scratch in learning to work, budget, maintain a home, and think for herself, will attach to a dependable but controlling partner for all the wrong reasons.

The third type of overindulgence is *Soft Structure*. Kids raised with too much freedom and without clearly communicated limits and expectations are likely to become socially irresponsible adults who don't feel obligated to live by the rules.

Interestingly, only 48% of those surveyed, who believe they were overindulged as kids, felt loved.

In general terms, an overindulged child is likely to miss the opportunity to learn to *delay gratification*: a necessary skill for adulthood and for appropriately managing anger. Let's take a look at an infant's ability to delay gratification.

He doesn't have any.

He wants what he wants when he wants it. His little lungs will work overtime, letting you know he's frustrated at not having his needs met, right up until the time that they are. It may be a bottle he wants, to be burped, or to have his diaper changed. Whatever the need, he's not about to be ignored. The infant is understandably dependent on his caregivers for survival, and they have a responsibility to respond to his every need. If they do not, the child will not learn to trust. Unable to trust, the child will likely face lifelong interpersonal struggles.

But as the child grows and is able to tend to more of his own needs, it is critical that he be allowed to do so. Furthermore, along the path to adulthood, he must learn that some things he might want will not come to him immediately; that before he can get to D, he must accomplish A, B, and C, and it may take some time and effort. Perhaps that new MP3 player will only come to him after he's mowed a number of neighborhood lawns over a number of weeks or even months. To expect to have D (the MP3) without A, B, and C (mowing lawns) is the posture of the helpless, dependent child. It is necessary for the adult caregiver to allow the growing child some frustration, in learning to delay gratification.

Now let's look at that same overindulged child 10 years later, lacking the ability to delay gratification. Imagine that he has been dumped by his girlfriend and he is in pain. He doesn't like being in pain and he wants it gone. While the adult who learned to delay gratification as a child might be willing to accept that pain and frustration is a part of life (and survivable), the adult overindulged as a child, may not. He may be unwilling to accept anything short of immediate relief. While the able child will accept allowing some time for healing and be willing to use some effective (if not immediately pain-freeing) coping strategies (say, talking with a friend, self-examination, exercise, staying busy), the overindulged child/adult is more likely to look for the quick 'fix'—maybe alcohol, other drugs, sex, or negative attention (by acting out inappropriately). Relying on these 'quick fixes' as a means of coping over time will oftentimes result in an adult seriously lacking in coping skills. An infant in a grown-up's body.

▶ A Case in Point (Frank's Therapy Client)

Frank once counseled a 30-year-old man we'll call Nick. An only child, showered with stuff, and allowed nearly total freedom to come and go without question, Nick was an overindulged child who began using marijuana as an anesthetic for emotional pain in his midteens. By the age of 18, he had graduated to cocaine. Amazingly bright and naturally talented in computers and electronics, but lacking the patience to finish college, Nick was nonetheless able to land a job with a major electronics manufacturer. By the age of 25, he had risen to a position of great responsibility, using cocaine every day along the way. Nick headed up a project for a major airline, designing and installing a very highly technical cockpit safety apparatus. But Nick's life had become unmanageable because of his 'painkilling' addiction to cocaine.

Frank first met Nick after he was admitted to a mental health facility where Frank led group therapy sessions. At the time of admission, he was paranoid and delusional. Nick refused to come out of his room for the first few days of his hospitalization. When he finally did, he refused to speak for over a week. When Nick finally began to open up, he told Frank that before he was admitted to the hospital he was convinced that he was being spied upon. He'd even installed a highly sophisticated listening device in the attic of his house to beat the bad guys at their own game. Overwhelmed and frightened, Nick's longtime live-in girlfriend had taken her adolescent daughter and moved out. Nick's drug-induced paranoia had taken over his life.

After his 4-week hospital stay, Frank began seeing Nick on an outpatient basis. Etched in Frank's memory is an early session with Nick, as he recalled being allowed to fly in the cockpit of a giant airliner, so that he could test the equipment he'd installed.

'It was so cool!' Nick exclaimed. 'The pilot was joking around with me, and I could look straight out the front window!'

Frank was struck by the unbridled glee of a young adolescent inside the body of a fully grown and brilliant man.

Therapy consisted of taking one life experience at a time and learning new coping skills to deal with that particular problem. Watching Nick grow, drug free, was like watching a weight lifter whose muscles grew before Frank's eyes with every single repetition. He seemed to develop, emotionally, from a 15-year-old (the time he started using drugs to cope) to a 20-year-old, in a matter of a few months. During that particular phase of his therapy, he told Frank that he was seriously considering leaving his job to look for work in a fast-food restaurant.

'You want to leave your high-tech job where you are highly respected and earning $90 000 a year, to flip burgers?' Frank asked.

'That's what I'm saying,' Nick told Frank. 'I just feel like that's where I should be working. I can't take it. My job is too stressful.'

Frank told Nick that he believed he wanted to work in a fast-food restaurant because he was still emotionally a teenager, or possibly a very young adult.

'What 20-year-old would want to cope with the stress and responsibility of your job?'

Nick agreed, and the insight was enough to keep him working in therapy . . . and in his job.

Six months later, now about a year into his recovery, Nick showed up for his session with a big smile on his face. He sat down, rolled up his sleeve, and proudly displayed a new brightly colored Superman tattoo. The comical superhero figure in blue tights and red cape looked strikingly like a caricature of Nick. At that moment, Frank knew that Nick was going to be all right.

Nick had managed to develop the coping skills he had missed out on during his teens, and he'd successfully learned to deal with the frustration that comes with having to delay gratification. Overindulged as a child and formerly unwilling to tolerate frustration, Nick had finally become an adult.

▶ Feeding the Good Wolf

Working in a helping profession in a small community can be an incredibly positive and fulfilling experience, or it can be a nightmare. Of particular importance is the degree of professionalism and dedication of one's colleagues. We've been fortunate to have had some wonderful colleagues over the years. One afternoon the local child protective services social worker knocked on Frank's office door. Kathy held a sheet of paper in her hand and she wanted Frank to have it. A week prior, she had referred a 12-year-old Native American boy and his father to Frank for counseling, after the dad had been arrested for alleged physical abuse of the boy. He was released 2 days later, after Kathy's investigation had revealed that the boy had gone into a rage, nearly destroying their home, and dad, who suffered from a severe neck injury that caused him chronic pain, had found it necessary to strike the boy on the leg with a small stick to keep him from attacking, or hurting himself.

Now Kathy handed Frank the page, which she had printed from an Internet sight. The title read, *Which Wolf Do You Feed*? Frank quickly learned the story was based on Cherokee lore, and was used to build character in kids. In the story, a Cherokee grandfather tells his grandson about a battle that goes on inside people. He said, 'My son, the battle is between two wolves inside us all.' One is evil, filled with anger, envy, jealousy, greed, arrogance, and ego. The other is good, filled with joy, peace, love, hope, empathy, and kindness. The grandson thought about this, then asked his grandfather, 'Which wolf wins?' The grandfather replied simply, 'the one you feed.'

Touched by the powerful traditional tale, Frank sought the help of a computer-savvy coworker to reprint the story and add a photo of a beautiful wolf in the wild. They found a suitable frame, and Frank presented it to his young client during his next session. They discussed the story, and Frank suggested he keep the piece in plain sight at home, to serve as a reminder to feed the good wolf.

In a modern society, food for the evil wolf can reach your child from many directions. Some of the more obvious come from violent movies and video games, vile and dehumanizing music lyrics, hate-mongering Internet sites, and mindless television programming. But beware the more subtle food for the evil wolf, and understand that what your child ingests for character building begins with *you*. Our society likes to rely on the 'do as I say, not as I do' rule, as a means of rationalizing our misbehavior and minimizing the imperfect role-modeling we offer to our kids. While we are certainly all less than perfect, let's be mindful that our kids are watching, and we're not allowed a free pass because we've asked them to pay attention to our words, and not to our actions. It's not going to happen.

That said, don't stop talking to your kids about doing the right thing. Notice we said *talking*; not lecturing. A young person will deal with lecturing for maybe 5 minutes before tuning us out. Talking with your child, on the other hand, is a highly effective way of teaching and *nurturing*, and nurturance is universally desired and accepted. The difference between lecturing and talking? Make it a conversation; a two-way exchange with a mutual understanding that both parties will be treated with respect in the process.

When you find yourself discouraged following a session of 'feeding the good wolf,' feeling that your child didn't hear a word you said, know that you've no doubt planted a seed. That seed is quite likely to bare fruit at some future time when it will truly make a difference in your child's life. Food for the good wolf. Particularly for those young wolves lacking in the necessary skills to identify, express, and manage anger.

Lastly, we have found the activities contained in this book to be invaluable for instilling vital principles of character in kids. We like to think of the workbook activities you will find in this book as prepackaged *Food for the Good Wolf*.

▶ Touching on Spirituality and Character

In *The Strength of Character* (2007), Charles Swindoll emphasizes his view that God wants to do mighty work in and through us, and he gives thanks to the '3-second pause,' the ability to wait 3 seconds before giving in to any impulse, no matter what the temptation. He writes that during those 3 seconds, he is able to anticipate what the consequences of his actions might be. Swindoll credits the 3-second pause for keeping him out of a lot of hot water over the course of his lifetime, and for helping him to establish self-control and develop character. For those readers interested in the neurobiology of the 3-second pause (what happens in the brain that makes those 3 seconds so very critical), see Chapter 2.

In discussing discipline, Swindoll writes about the need to enslave the body; like an athlete showing his body who is boss. 'That includes its every whining wish that we indulge its every whim. The point of disciplined self-control is to make the body serve us rather than the other way around' (p. 49).

How important is religion in developing character? In *A Course in Life* (1998), author Joan Gattuso writes about the importance of adhering to universal spiritual laws if we are to achieve personal fulfillment in our lives. Spiritual laws are as reliable as the laws that govern our physical world: laws such as gravity, the consistency of the angles of a triangle adding up to 180 degrees, and the speed of light remaining at 186 000 miles per hour. Whether we understand them or not, physical laws are always at work. Their working is not dependent on our understanding. According to Gattuso, the same is true of the spiritual laws governing our spiritual lives. 'If we accept that we are spiritual beings having a human experience, we can discover and attune ourselves to these demonstrable Spiritual Principles, which always work' (p. 9).

In the classic, *The Road Less Traveled* (1978), psychiatrist M. Scott Peck writes that most people who struggle in their lives to the point of eventually seeking out psychotherapy are either neurotic or character disordered. He boils both mental health problems down to a problem with *responsibility*. Neurotics, Peck claims, take too much responsibility, blaming themselves for problems that aren't theirs, while those with character disorders refuse to take responsibility for their problems and blame others.

A seemingly simplistic code of conduct for being good to ourselves and others, and achieving personal freedom is offered up by physician and Toltec healer Don Miguel Ruiz in *The Four Agreements* (1997).

First off, Ruiz recommends we Be Impeccable with Our Word. The idea here is to say only what we mean and to avoid using words to hurt others or ourselves, such as when we gossip or put ourselves down.

Next is, Don't Take Anything Personally. How others respond to us is a projection of their own reality, and nothing that others do is because of us.

The third agreement is Don't Make Assumptions. Believing we understand the intentions of others without checking it out is too often a recipe for disaster. When we have the courage to communicate with others as clearly as we can, we can avoid misunderstandings and drama.

Lastly, Always Do Your Best. Accomplish this from day to day and we will avoid self-judgment, self-abuse, and regret.

These character-conscious rules to live by may seem simple, but to accomplish them takes courage and commitment. Striving toward these goals, even if we fall short, is bound to have a positive effect on our lives and the lives of those around us. We highly recommend *The Four Agreements* be a topic of discussion when talking about character with your kids.

▶ Considering 'Intergenerational Poverty'

It's far too easy for middle-class teachers, counselors, and other helping professionals to judge the character of those who live in poverty. When these kids miss a lot of school, or are repeated no-shows for counseling appointments, our tendency as professionals is to assume that these kids and their parents are failing to take responsibility and just don't care. We may even go as far as to decide that this same lack of character and initiative is the reason they are poor in the first place.

To make these judgments is to be ignorant to the realities of intergenerational poverty. While the middle class has the luxury of motoring from one place to another—lunch with friends, a PTA meeting, the dentist for the annual cleaning, a Saturday round of golf with coworkers—the family in poverty is likely preoccupied with how to get Aunt Emily, who has been in pain for days and now can't stand, to the nearest emergency room. And if tending to this crisis conflicts with keeping an appointment or showing up at school, Aunt Emily is going to win out every time.

The only person in the extended family with a car that runs, this individual has been raised in intergenerational poverty; where focus on the future is limited to surviving one day at a time, and one's first obligation is to the extended family members. In the scheme of things, getting Aunt Emily to the hospital is of much higher priority than keeping a counseling appointment or making a parent–teacher conference. To not be there for the immediate needs of the family and community is to risk not having their assistance at a time of crisis, and therefore a risk to personal survival.

While the middle-class professional may see the solution to intergenerational poverty to be long-term planning—finishing school, attending college, getting a steady job, opening a savings account, and saving for retirement—the person *living* in intergenerational poverty is focused on getting through the day. To focus elsewhere is to put one's survival and the survival of the family at risk.

The school-age child living in intergenerational poverty is likely to be sharing a home with an 8- to 12-member extended family, or community members. He is likely to hone his aggressive tendencies in order to get his share, and a quiet place to complete is homework is in most cases out of the question.

The responsibility of the middle-class professional service provider (counselor, teacher, public services worker, etc.) first and foremost, is to gain some insight into the life and mindset of the individual and family living in intergenerational poverty, then to help them obtain the services of competent service providers who also understand their plight. Most important is to not confuse a person's character with what they must do to survive. Character is not dependent on social class.

We are reminded of the story of Charles Plumb, a US Navy jet pilot who was shot down over Vietnam after 75 combat missions, and spent 6 years in a Vietnamese prison. One day, while seated in a restaurant, Plumb was approached by a man who recognized him. 'You're Plumb. You flew jets from the Kitty Hawk, and were shot down!'

Plumb was shocked that anyone would recognize him so many years after his military service.

'How did you know that?' asked Plumb.

'I packed your parachute,' the man answered.

Plumb gasped and shook the man's hand in gratitude, 'I guess it worked!'

Plumb later wondered how many times he had seen the young sailor in his bellbottom trousers and white hat, and never even said 'Good morning.' You see, Plumb had been a fighter pilot and the man who packed his chute, just a sailor. He thought of the many hours the sailor must have spent standing at a long wooden table in the bowels of the ship, carefully weaving the shrouds and folding the silks of each chute, holding in his hands the lives of men he didn't know.

Who's packing your parachute?

◀ CHAPTER FIVE ▶

The Labeling of Children: When Anger Leads to Diagnosis

You've got to have something to eat and a little love in you before you can hold still for any damn body's sermon on how to behave.
— Billie Holiday, American singer (1915–1959)

The child lacking in the skills needed to identify, process, and appropriately express anger is, far too frequently, eventually diagnosed with a mental health disorder. The most common labels pinned to angry kids include oppositional defiant disorder (ODD) and attention-deficit hyperactivity disorder (ADHD). Others include bipolar disorder and conduct disorder.

The labeling of children goes against our better instincts, mainly because we respect and appreciate the individuality of each child. But if there is usefulness to the diagnosing of kids, it is that doing so may improve our ability to help the child develop, learn, and relate to others in a healthy way. Simply put, a diagnosis is nothing more than a label placed on a child, based on a set of observable or otherwise verifiable behaviors or other types of symptoms, which may or may not be biologically based (a brain problem). If a counselor, teacher, or parent knows from training or experience that a particular set of problem behaviors or symptoms will respond positively to certain types of care or treatment, then the diagnosis might be useful in helping to alleviate the child's struggles and emotional pain.

In some cases, this label placed on a child, based on a grouping of symptoms, is sufficient motivation to involve a medical doctor such as a pediatrician or child psychiatrist in the child's care, particularly when these symptoms or behaviors may pose a danger to the child or those around him.

We recognize the reluctance of many clinicians, ourselves included, to pin kids with diagnostic labels, particularly at a very young age. It's quite common for a mental health clinician to take the 'compassionate out.' That is, to go with the less 'serious,' less stigmatizing diagnosis. For example, a child that may indeed meet the criteria for conduct disorder, if just barely, might be diagnosed with ODD. In the case of a child exhibiting symptoms of an autism spectrum disorder such as Asperger's syndrome, an unwilling-to-stigmatize clinician might initially label that child with pervasive developmental disorder, NOS (not otherwise specified). The rationale for doing so may include the idea that a diagnosis can always be changed, in this case, 'upgraded' to the more 'serious' one, if the symptoms become more pronounced or the stigmatizing diagnosis is more obviously substantiated over time. A notable child psychologist and colleague who specializes in treating kids with autism recently told us that he constantly had to refer kids back to clinicians who were inclined to take the compassionate out. Understandably, he was concerned that his treatment was too frequently not matching up with the initial diagnosis. Once in his care, he was convinced that the more serious diagnosis was justified, and he was ethically bound to provide the required treatment.

SmartHelp for Good 'n' Angry Kids. By Frank Jacobelli and Lynn Ann Watson
© 2009 Blackwell Publishing, ISBN 978-0-470-75802-1

Is taking the compassionate out ever a good idea, or does it simply serve the clinician by allowing him or her to avoid the anxiety-producing task of diagnosing a young child with a serious and/or difficult-to-treat diagnosis?

We subscribe to the principle that if the more serious, difficult-to-treat diagnosis isn't *quite obviously* substantiated by the child's symptoms and behaviors, it is legitimately less-stigmatizing to use the 'lesser' diagnosis, at least initially. While the lesser diagnosis is easily upgraded by entering the additional behavioral criteria into the child's medical record, removing the stigma of having once been labeled with a serious and difficult-to-treat diagnosis may follow that child for a lifetime.

That said, the clinician needs to be very careful not to 'under-diagnose' the child who will only receive the level of care that the more stigmatizing diagnosis will allow for, whether because of insurance reimbursement, the need for a medication evaluation, criteria for admission to a specialized treatment program, or for other reasons.

Given we contend that inappropriately expressed anger is often a result of unresolved hurt and a lack of the tools for coping with the resulting frustration, we need to be mindful of what we teach our kids about anger, its causes and usefulness. As a society, we have frequently sent our kids the message that ANGER is one letter from DANGER, and MAD, one letter from BAD. Too often the result is a child, aware of his 'anger issues,' considering himself defective or 'crazy,' only adding to his heartbreak.

While the child having difficulty expressing anger is not necessarily suffering from a mental health disorder, many of these kids are eventually pinned with one or more unflattering labels. To provide you, the reader, with a better understanding of what goes into the diagnosing of a child with a mental health disorder, we have included a general overview of the more common labels handed out to kids. In our experience, the most frequent diagnosis handed out to angry kids is that of ODD.

▶ Oppositional Defiant Disorder

While every child is oppositional at times, not every angry child should be labeled with ODD. Oppositional behavior may be the result of children testing limits in order to become more autonomous, test their personal power, or to have a clearer sense of themselves and their place in the world. 'Normal' kids have been known to talk back, disobey, argue, and even defy the authority of parents and teachers, particularly when tired, stressed, bored, or hungry. Only when there is an ongoing pattern of hostile and defiant behavior toward adults in authority, which significantly interferes with the child's ability to function day to day, might the child meet the clinical criteria for the mental health diagnosis of ODD.

ODD is diagnosed about twice as frequently as ADHD, and 5–15% of children and adolescents in the United States fully meet the criteria for the ODD diagnosis, as compared to 3–5% of kids labeled with ADHD. The oppositional defiant child is about three times more likely to be male than female.

The mental health clinician's current bible for diagnosing psychiatric disorders in the United States is the Diagnostic and Statistical Manual (fourth edition, text revised), commonly referred to as the DSM-IV-TR. (The ICD 10, produced by the World Health Organization, is most frequently used for diagnosing in Europe.) According to DSM-IV-TR, the essential feature of ODD is 'a recurrent pattern of negativistic, defiant, disobedient, and hostile behavior toward authority figures that persists for at least six months' (p. 100). Other criteria need to be present before the diagnosis can be correctly made, such as deliberately doing things that annoy other people, defying or refusing to follow the rules of adults, being vindictive, or blaming others. The truly ODD child is often stubborn and argumentative, and frequently tests the limits set by adults.

To be diagnosed with ODD, the child must exhibit these problem behaviors at rates higher than expected for children of similar developmental level, and the problems must cause clinically significant impairment in social or academic functioning. Readers interested in more detailed criteria for diagnosis of ODD should refer to the DSM-IV-TR or speak with a pediatrician or a mental health professional who specializes in diagnosing and treating children.

While the causes of ODD are not certain, and most likely multidimensional, over a hundred studies have shown that kids can become immune to the horrors of violence and may gradually accept aggression as a way of keeping stimulated and solving problems. Research supports the argument that the rate and content of stimulation in movies, television, and video games contribute to increased behavioral problems. A 2001 study conducted by the American Academy of Pediatrics concluded that the children who frequently watched wrestling on television were more likely to engage in fighting and other behaviors that put their health at risk. The same study concluded that children and teens who frequently watched violence on television were more likely to carry guns and other weapons, drive after drinking alcohol, and use stimulant medication not prescribed for them.

In 1961, Albert Bandura conducted the famous Bobo doll experiment, which supported the theory that children imitate the violence they see on television. In the experiment, children watched an adult play with a collection of toys that included an inflatable doll named Bobo, which the adult would now and then hit in the head with a rubber mallet. A separate group of children watched an adult play with the same toys, but who didn't hit Bobo with the mallet. After some time, each child was placed into a room filled with toys, including Bobo the doll. The children that had watched the adult act violently toward the doll repeated the behavior, while the other children did not. Believers in Bandura's conclusion that children who watch violence are more prone to commit violence are likely to cringe at the following statistic: a child who watches television 3 hours per day will have witnessed 200 000 violent acts by age 18 (Perry 2004).

Additionally, some studies have implicated abnormalities in the brain's prefrontal cortex in kids with ODD, leading some to believe the disorder to be at least partially 'brain-based' (Raine 2002).

Treatment for ODD generally consists of behavior modification and family therapy. As there is often an overlapping diagnosis, such as ADHD, other treatments, such as stimulant medication, are sometimes used in treating the ODD-diagnosed child. Specialized parenting courses and support groups can be useful in supporting parents in their efforts to implement effective behavior modifying practices at home.

▶ Trauma and Violence in the Lives of Children

A 2001 study conducted at Lehigh University concluded that preschool children who received severe physical discipline were more likely to become overly aggressive during their school years. Violence and emotional abuse at home have long been considered to be contributing factors in behavioral problems in children, even if the child is not the direct target of the abuse.

The authors had the pleasure of attending a lecture conducted by Bruce Perry, director of the Child Trauma Academy and an internationally recognized authority on brain development of children in crisis, in 2004. Dr Perry confirmed for us that traumatic stress in children, be it as a result of parental abuse or the horrors of trying to survive in a war-torn environment, has a direct result on the physical development of the brain, and leads to the development of a violent, remorseful child.

Perry contends that, because of the chaotic and undersocialized environment to which the child is exposed, the frontal lobes of these kids' brains (the most highly evolved part of the brain, responsible for resisting impulses, seeing the big picture and thinking things through) are poorly organized. At the same time, the severe stress to which the child is exposed causes the 'reptilian' (brainstem) part of the brain to function abnormally. Perry writes, 'This experience-based imbalance predisposes to a host of neuropsychiatric problems and violent behavior' (2007).

The authors want to emphasize the importance of a safe, peaceful, and nurturing environment for every child. Anything less puts the children at risk for emotional and behavioral problems that may or may not be 'brain-based,' in the end, depriving the children of their birthright to reach their full, human potential. Perry writes, 'The neurobiology of complex, heterogeneous behaviors is complex and heterogeneous. In the end, paying attention to neurobiologic impact of developmental experiences—traumatic or nurturing—will yield great insight for prevention and therapeutic interventions.' About 5 million children in the United States are exposed to some form of traumatic violence each year, child abuse and domestic violence being the two most common forms of trauma in the lives of kids (Perry 1999).

In common sense terms, whether or not violence is present at home, a child may be lacking necessary support and guidance. If we want kids to have the kinds of skills taught in this book, somebody's going to have to teach them. Because you have this book in front of you, it's a safe bet that you agree. For that we are both grateful . . . and hopeful.

▶ Attention-Deficit/Hyperactivity Disorder

Our experience has taught us that kids diagnosed with ADHD frequently have difficulty managing anger as a result of their frustration with trying to meet the expectations of others. Whether in the classroom or at home, these kids have difficulty paying attention and/or managing impulses and are frequently in violation of someone's rules. As a result, they are often reprimanded and in other ways are targets of negative attention. The child who is responsible for holding up a classroom activity because of these behaviors, for example, may be labeled a 'troublemaker' by teachers and classmates alike. This often leads to a negative self-image and the fulfilling of one's own expectations with a pattern of negative behavior.

Because the ADHD-labeled child generally has difficulty learning, he often underperforms in relation to his classmates, resulting in additional frustration when inevitably comparing his academic accomplishments to those of his peers. Additionally, the impulsive, hyperactive child typically has problems getting along with peers, often feeling disliked and alone. These learning, behavior, and social problems frequently combine and result in a tense and resentful child, looking for a reason to let loose. The DSM-IV-TR, published by the American Psychiatric Association, describes the essential feature of ADHD as 'a persistent pattern of inattention and/or hyperactivity-impulsivity that is more frequently displayed and more severe than is typically observed in individuals at a comparable level of development' (p. 85). In addition to this essential feature, the diagnosis cannot be made unless there are other criteria met, including clear evidence of interference in social, academic, or occupational functioning, and some of the symptoms must be present before age 7.

A child labeled with ADHD often shifts his attention from one uncompleted task to another and has trouble paying attention to detail. The child's work is frequently performed without much thought and is often messy, and he has an easier time paying attention to novel and/or highly stimulating activities, than those that are repetitive or less exciting. This child will generally avoid activities that require sustained attention or much mental effort. The authors of have taken this fact into consideration in creating the activities contained in the workbooks.

Children with ADHD may have a hard time staying in their seat, even when leaving their seat would be breaking the rules, such as in the classroom. The DSM-IV-TR describes this person as one appearing to be 'driven by a motor.' Hyperactivity is frequently present in ADHD, but not always. Impulsivity is also frequent, but not always part of the behavioral picture. When present, it is generally in the form of a kind of pressure to act, react, or speak, even when not doing so would be more socially appropriate and lead to fewer unwanted consequences. In order for a person to be diagnosed with ADHD, there must be impairment in the ability to function in at least two settings, such as at school, home, work, or in social situations.

Prior to 1994 and publication of the DSM-IV, the American Psychiatric Association considered attention deficit disorder (ADD) and ADHD to be two separate disorders. However, with the publication of DSM-IV, both came under the heading of ADHD. Additionally, three subtypes were added, depending on the type symptoms the individual is experiencing. In the *combined type*, both significant inattention and hyperactivity/impulsivity are present. The *predominantly inattentive type* is characterized mostly by problems in paying attention. When most of the problems involve hyperactivity/impulsivity, the *predominantly hyperactive type* is diagnosed (American Psychiatric Association 2000). Rather than rely on this simplified summary of ADHD criteria, readers should review the DSM-IV-TR criteria for themselves, or better still, have a discussion with a qualified pediatrician or child therapist.

The most common medical treatment of ADHD involves the use of stimulant medication. There are currently four stimulant medications that have been on the market for treating kids with ADHD for 20 years or longer. They include Ritalin (methylphenidate), Dexedrine (dextroamphetamine), Adderall (amphetamine-dextroamphetamine), and Cylert (pemoline). Though controversial, research indicates stimulant medication is often effective in lessening the symptoms of ADHD in kids (Greenhill, Halperin, and Abikoff 1999).

Nonmedical treatments of ADHD include behavior modification, social skills training, and family therapy. Neurotherapy and neurofeedback have shown effectiveness in changing particular brainwave patterns that are often present in children diagnosed with ADHD (Hammond 2005). The authors of this book have found that symptoms of ADHD kids can be lessened by helping them to 'exercise' their prefrontal cortex, using specific workbook activities that present lessons specific to the individual child's particular learning strengths and interests (Jacobelli and Watson 2008).

▶ Attention-Deficit Hyperactivity Disorder in Question

Interestingly, even the experts in the field disagree as to whether ADHD truly even exists. In a training several years ago, led by a clinical psychologist specializing in children's behavior problems, we were taken aback by the instructor's resolve in commenting, 'the labeling of kids with ADHD is the result of nothing more that a child being more active than someone else wants him to be.' This reputable psychologist is not alone in his thinking.

Convinced that the ADD diagnosis became tremendously popular in the 1990s because it was a convenient way to explain away the complexities of American life toward the end of the twentieth century, Thomas Armstrong discounts the existence of the disorder. He writes, 'when our children begin to act out under strain, it's convenient to create a scientific-sounding term to label them with, and a whole program of workbooks, videos, and instructional materials to use to fit them in a box that relieves parents and teachers of any worry that it might be due to their own failure (or the failure of a broader culture) to nurture or to teach effectively' (1997). Armstrong credits societal factors such as the breakdown of the family, mass media's creation of a short-attention-span culture, the erosion of respect for the family, and intensified stress levels for the learning and behavior problems that frequently result in the ADHD diagnosis in children.

Another highly respected nonbeliever is the best-selling author and Executive Director of the Children's Success Foundation, Howard Glasser. In *101 Reasons to Avoid Ritalin like the Plague* (2005), Glasser opposes the labeling and medicating of intense children. Among the 100 reasons for avoiding Ritalin, cited by Glasser, is #40: 'Children feel fear when they sense that their parents can't handle them. They do not receive the modeling of a healthy sense of power; they see the parents giving up, surrendering to using drugs to control their behavior' (p. 60).

On the opposing side of the argument is Dr Russell Barkley, who wrote the book on ADHD, *Attention-Deficit Hyperactivity Disorder* (1998). He refers to kids meeting the diagnostic criteria for ADHD as having a disorder of self-control, oftentimes overwhelmed by their own energy and intensity. Barkley notes that 10–20% of kids diagnosed with ADHD and put on medication show no real improvement, and even when the medication appears to be helping, the side effects prove to be too difficult for many children. A third group of children, according to Barkley, are those whose parents decide not to seriously consider medication for their children.

Sharing the viewpoint that ADHD is a brain-based disorder, often improved with medication, is Dr Daniel Amen, who not only believes that the disorder exists, but believes he has the pictures to prove it (see Chapter 2). In fact, Amen identifies six separate types of ADD in his book *Healing ADD: The Breakthrough Program That Allows You to See and Heal the 6 Types of ADD* (2001); all six types, Amen claims, can be identified using SPECT scan technology.

▶ The 'Numbing-Down' of Your Child's Brain

Although it has become increasingly clear that trauma in the lives of children, and exposure to violence, can shape the brain in such a way that the child may be predisposed to violence, there is evidence that the amount of overwhelming stimulation experienced by kids today is also changing their brains. The Rational Psychology Association in Munich, Germany, conducted a 20-year study, examining the effects of technology on the brain. The study, which looked at 4000 subjects every 5 years, found that it was becoming more and more difficult to stimulate the brain's cerebral cortex.

The association concluded that sensitivity to stimuli in these kids is steadily decreasing, at a rate of about 1% per year. The report found that 'as visual stimuli goes in, entire areas of the brain are being skipped over, and this optical information is being processed without actually being evaluated' (Stevens 2007). It may be that due to the deluge of stimulation to which children are being exposed, they may be able to watch violent television and video and play gruesome video games without experiencing emotion. As a result, kids may be learning to only pay attention if it's extremely exciting and stimulating.

It may be that a 'new brain' has been developed for any of us born after 1969, as a result of the technology boom and exposure of our kids to the highly pleasurable but overwhelming stimulation delivered by video games, action movies, and 24-hour real-time and repetitive coverage of disasters, car chases, and violent crimes. The brain dulled-down by this 'mind-numbing' stimulation is likely attached to a child unsatisfied by what those of us born before 1969 would find adequately and enjoyably stimulating. A logical conclusion may be that the ODD- or ADHD-labeled child, or the undiagnosed but angry child, is neurologically prone to impatience, ever on the lookout for what is adequately stimulating, regardless of the expectations of the adults in charge.

▶ Bipolar Disorder

Historically, a diagnosis of bipolar disorder was rarely made in anyone under the age of 18, but it seems diagnosing children with bipolar illness has become all the rage in the early years of the twenty-first century. As a result, there exists a schism in the mental health field with regard to the prevalence of bipolar disorder in children and adolescents. According to the Depression and Bipolar Support Alliance, 'up to one-third of the 3.4 million children and adolescents with depression in the United States may actually be experiencing the early onset of bipolar illness' (www.dbsalliance.org). By some estimates, there may be as many as 1 million kids under the age of 18 suffering from bipolar illness (Wagemaker 2003).

Is there an epidemic of bipolar disorder in kids, or are kids simply being overdiagnosed?

Bipolar illness is a serious mental illness characterized by recurrent episodes of depression, mania, and/or mixed symptom states. The individual is likely to experience extreme shifts in mood, energy, and behavior that interfere significantly with normal functioning. But existing evidence indicates that bipolar illness that begins in childhood or early adolescence may be different from bipolar illness beginning in adulthood. In kids, the illness may present as continuous, rapid cycling, irritable or mixed symptom states, and the disorder may co-occur with other disruptive disorders such as attention-deficit/hyperactivity disorder or conduct disorder (described later). Maintaining a normal sleep pattern is often troublesome in bipolar kids, and they often have trouble getting going in the morning. A lack of sleep may correlate with the onset of mania. The bipolar child tends to have difficulty getting started in the morning, and may be able to function more capably by noon time.

A child or adolescent, who appears to be depressed and exhibits severe ADHD-like symptoms with excessive temper tantrums and mood changes, should be evaluated by a licensed mental health professional, particularly if there is a family history of bipolar disorder. A child psychiatrist with a good deal of experience evaluating and treating bipolar illness would be a good choice.

A word of caution here—effective treatment of bipolar illness in kids begins with an accurate diagnosis. Because symptoms of the illness in children and adolescents often differ from those seen in adults, it's critical to obtain the best possible care from the onset. For example, there is some evidence that taking anti-depressant drugs without a mood-stabilizing medication may actually cause a manic episode in an individual with bipolar disorder. Likewise, if mistakenly diagnosed with ADHD, the taking of stimulant medication may worsen mania in a child with bipolar illness.

A child with one bipolar parent has a 10–30% chance of becoming bipolar. The likelihood jumps to 75% if both parents are bipolar. In nearly all cases, the bipolar child has a close relative with the disorder.

The truly bipolar but untreated child may be at risk. The mood instability, depression, mania, and agitation can lead to dangerous, even life-threatening behaviors. The child will likely require the ongoing medication management that only a child psychiatrist, highly experienced pediatrician, or pediatric neurologist can provide. In *Psychiatric Medications and our Children* (2003), Herbert Wagemaker writes that the mood-stabilizing drug, Lithium, has been approved for treating adolescents, but not children, and some studies have found the drug to be effective in lessening the symptoms of bipolar illness in teens. Side effects of the medication can include tremor, fatigue, weight gain, and nausea. Less commonly, more serious side effects involve the thyroid gland, kidneys, heart, and skin. As is often the case when medicating children, with so much life ahead of them, a realistic concern is that the long-term side effects may not emerge until the child is much older.

Additionally, cognitive-behavioral therapy has been shown to be useful, as is family therapy for helping the family unit to cope. The activities contained herein can serve as a valuable addition to treatment as well.

▶ Conduct Disorder

Considered more serious than Oppositional Defiant Disorder, and possibly not 'brain-based,' children who meet the criteria for a diagnosis of conduct disorder repeatedly violate the personal or property rights of others and the basic expectations of society. The diagnosis requires that the child or adolescent's symptoms continue for 6 months or longer.

Frequently, children who develop conduct disorder had at some time in the past been diagnosed with ODD. About 1–4% of kids aged 9 to 17 are affected by conduct disorder. The disorder is more common in cities than in rural areas, and affects boys more often than girls.

Symptoms of conduct disorder include the following: (1) aggressive behavior that harms or threatens others or animals, (2) behavior that damages or destroys property, (3) lying or stealing, (4) truancy or other serious rule violations, (5) early tobacco, alcohol, other substance use, (6) precocious sexual activity.

In some cases, conduct disorder first appears in the preschool years, but more commonly first presents when the child is older. Some children who are particularly 'fussy' infants appear to be at risk for developing the behaviors that can lead to a diagnosis of conduct disorder.

Some factors that may make a child more likely to develop conduct disorder include early maternal rejection, family neglect, abuse or exposure to violence, and poverty.

While conduct disorder is often difficult to treat, parents can benefit from specialized training on dealing with their child's behaviors. Family therapy and training in problem-solving skills may also benefit the child and family. Medication is not typically prescribed for conduct disorder, unless a significant depression or ADHD component has been identified.

▶ Seeing Each Child in Context

We can't emphasize strongly enough the importance of seeing and treating each child as an individual. Whether your child is 'diagnosable' or not, he or she is not the same as anyone else on the planet. It's important to recognize the individual learning style and strengths of the child you are trying to help, certainly, but learning strengths are only one aspect of each child's individuality. Let's take the case of Simon.

Simon is a bright, 10-year-old fourth-grader and he's having a tough day. Not a strong verbal-linguistic learner, Simon's least favorite time of day is after lunch when his teacher passes out a list of vocabulary words for each student to define. Simon has learned from experience that he is usually the last to finish, and his vocabulary scores are consistently below the class average.

A strong bodily-kinesthetic learner, Simon is aware of his body, how it feels, and how to use it. As his teacher passes out the vocabulary sheets, Simon easily notices a sick feeling in his stomach, and his palms begin to sweat. Fifteen minutes later, Simon's teacher wants to know who has completed the assignment and asks for a show of hands. The only student still struggling with defining the list of words is Simon and he is mortified. Overwhelmed by recent budget cuts, a shortage of supplies, and the demands of an overfilled class, Simon's teacher is out of patience.

'Simon! Are we going to have to wait for you again!'

Heart racing now, muscles coiled and ready to strike, Simon blows it! He tears his paper in half, makes it into a ball and lets it fly in the direction of his teacher. Five minutes later, Simon finds himself in front of the principal and hangs his head. Overwhelmed by the school district's fiscal crisis and complaining teachers and pressure from the school board to improve test scores, Simon's principal is, himself, overwhelmed.

'I have no time to waste on unruly students who have nothing better to do than throw tantrums!' the principal shouts at Simon. 'Now you sit there quietly and think about why you were disrespectful to your teacher.'

Simon sits quietly, but the only sense he can make of his own behavior is that he must be a *bad* kid, and Simon's self-esteem crumbles.

Not only have Simon's teacher and principal failed to consider his difficulty learning verbal-linguistically or his strong bodily-kinesthetic learning style, but they also know nothing about Simon's life.

After his parents' recent and bitter divorce, Simon and his mother were forced to move to a small apartment in a run-down part of the town. The neighborhood kids have been bullying Simon because of his nice clothes and because they know he came from the 'rich' side of town. He has been in three fights in as many weeks and he hasn't told his mother for fear of adding to her worries. Simon's mother has taken a second job and he is often alone after school until his mother tucks him in at night, after finally getting home from work. Simon is aware of the terrible bitterness between his parents, and he worries that his father will soon decide to just stay away, and he will never see him again.

Simon's mother finally insisted on a divorce after years of intimidation and verbal abuse by his father. Unskilled in dealing with his feelings, his dad resorted to yelling and throwing things to vent his frustration. Simon's mother had eventually begun to fear for her safety and that of her son.

Simon desperately lacked a healthy role model for learning about feelings, expressing anger, and solving interpersonal problems. Well-meaning, his mother had been preoccupied for years, trying just to appease her angry husband.

Without help, what is likely to become of Simon?

The mounting pressure in his life and lack of support is likely to lead to more frequent episodes of extreme frustration expressed inappropriately, even destructively. His teachers and principal will likely write Simon off as a troublemaker, and divert what time and attention they have to offer, elsewhere. Simon will likely begin to believe the spoken and unspoken opinions of him, and continue to live up to his reputation as a troubled, angry child. Lacking attention from his parents, the negative attention he receives as a result of his behavior, he may decide, is better than no attention at all.

What can be done to help turn things around for Simon? First, Simon's teacher or principal might remind Simon that he is a bright student and that this angry behavior is unlike him, and take a few minutes to listen. She could phone his mother or ask for a meeting. By doing so, Simon's teacher and principal will have the opportunity to learn a little bit about what Simon is going through in his life, and be less likely to make assumptions or pass judgments. Perhaps Simon's mother will decide that Simon might benefit from meeting with the school counselor, for help in sorting out his feelings, getting support, and solving problems.

Next, Simon should be given the opportunity to learn about feelings and what to do with them. With practice and the support of others, he will be able to replace the inappropriate ways he has been using to express anger with healthy and appropriate ones, the kind contained in the workbooks in this book.

Third, Simon should be given the opportunity to learn about his learning style. A wonderful way to do this is in the classroom, where each student can learn about the ways they learn best, and develop an appreciation for the learning styles of others. When it is time for the class to divide into groups and complete a science or art project, which requires the skills of a hands-on bodily-kinesthetic learner, Simon will have the opportunity to shine. And the other kids will begin to learn that one learning style isn't better than another, just different. We strongly recommend the use of this book in your child's classroom.

Simon is not yet a 'diagnosable' child, in need of a label. He *is* understandably stressed and lacking in the skills it takes to manage his feelings in a healthy way. Furthermore, he happens to be a strong bodily-kinesthetic learner who loves to make things, play sports, dance, and push himself in physical ways that others can't. But because he is less strong than his classmates in the verbal-linguistic style of learning, the style most highly regarded in modern society, he is prone to frustration in the classroom, unless his teacher takes the time to understand learning styles and value each child as an individual.

Because he is in touch with his body and the way it works, he may more easily learn to use these skills in managing anger, than will most kids. He may be better able to pay attention to his body's early warning signs that anger is brewing. Then, with practice, he can learn to counteract his growing anger by deep-breathing or relaxing his muscles or both. Or, he might be taught that a good run before things get out of hand is just the ticket for heading off destructive anger. Until Simon, his mother, and his teacher are aware of how Simon learns best, he will likely be unable to draw on these bodily-kinesthetic means of expressing anger appropriately, and without negative consequences.

Whether determined to help a child labeled ODD, ADHD, 'difficult,' stressed, or just plain *angry*, the activities in this book have been invaluable for teaching the skills necessary for lessening the excessive and destructive anger in the children we've taught and counseled. We are confident they will do the same for your child.

◀ CHAPTER SIX ▶

Reaching and Teaching the Angry Child—And How to Stay Sane in the Process

Don't worry that children never listen to you. Worry that they are always watching you.
— Robert Fulghum, American author (b. 1937)

Parents of ADHD kids are three times more likely to become divorced than is the general population (Amen 2001). And while the majority of kids with anger problems are not ADHD, and shouldn't be 'labeled' as such, the survival of the family of the *angry* child is no less at risk. Teachers and counselors of angry kids are at heightened risk for the burnout that often comes with work-related chronic stress.

▶ The Moffets

Brad and Julie Moffet met in college and have been married for 13 years. Brad works as a department manager for a manufacturing company. Until recently, Julie worked as a property manager for a real estate company. Though she enjoyed her job and was on the fast-track toward promotion, the Moffets decided that Julie needed to be at home with their 9-year-old son, Jeff.

The younger of their two children, Jeff began having anger problems while still a toddler. Often restless and hard to console, his reaction to not getting his way was far more emotional and longer lasting than had been the reactions of Molly Moffet at Jeff's age. In kindergarten, Jeff had a hard time following instructions and was easily frustrated by his classmates. Once angered, Jeff seemed to quickly lose control, his anger escalating into a full-blown tirade. In a parent conference, Jeff's principal informed Brad and Julie that Jeff had become a classroom management problem for his teacher, and he asked if things were okay at home.

At home, Jeff is consuming more and more of his parents' time and energy. Brad and Julie feel as though they are walking on egg shells with Jeff, fearing that any reasonable attempt to discipline or set an appropriate limit will send him into an inconsolable rage. Among their fears is the possibility that Jeff will hurt himself or his sister, while overcome by his volcanic anger. Eleven-year-old Molly, once active and happy, has seemingly gone inside herself, often sulking and easily reduced to tears.

The Moffets wisely consulted with Jeff's pediatrician who examined Jeff and talked at length with his parents, but could find no physical cause for his intense anger. She informed Brad and Julie that Jeff didn't meet all of the criteria necessary to be diagnosed with ADHD, but asked that they consider a trial of Ritalin. Brad and Julie were reluctant to begin Jeff on

SmartHelp for Good 'n' Angry Kids. By Frank Jacobelli and Lynn Ann Watson
© 2009 Blackwell Publishing, ISBN 978-0-470-75802-1

stimulant medication, but agreed to discuss the possibility. The pediatrician recommended that Brad and Julie consider taking Jeff to a therapist specializing in the treatment of kids with behavior problems. She also suggested that family therapy might be helpful.

The decision was made for Julie to quit her job, reducing the family income by nearly half, and creating an unwelcome financial strain. More devastating was the guilt that Brad and Julie felt about their young son's apparent unhappiness. How had they failed him as parents?

Brad and Julie began to bicker over each other's parenting techniques, and each felt accused by the other of having damaged their son in some irreversible way. They argued over how money was spent, and agonized over how they would manage to pay for a child and family therapist on their recently reduced income.

In the ensuing months, Brad has begun to volunteer for overtime on his job, explaining to Julie that the extra hours would help the family financially. In truth, Brad would often prefer to be anywhere but home. Julie has begun to feel resentful, having given up her job to be home with Jeff. The Moffets' marriage is in trouble.

What can be done for Jeff?

▶ Making a Plan

While Jeff's behavioral problems appear to be happening in all settings, the school district is often the best place to begin requesting help. In most states, the school districts have a responsibility to evaluate kids with learning and/or behavioral problems that interfere with learning. Therefore, these same districts commonly employ a special educator. In many districts, a school counselor, behavioral specialist, or school psychologist might also be an available resource. The goal of soliciting help from the school district should be for purposes of assessment, and for an educational and/or behavioral plan for helping Jeff to overcome his behavioral challenges, particularly as they impact upon his ability to learn in school.

The Moffets' first instinct to seek medical care from Jeff's pediatrician was a good one—allowing a medical doctor, specializing in kids, to rule out an underlying medical cause for the behavior. Once referred for special education services, the special educator should request a report from Jeff's pediatrician for his file. Jeff's parents should have a copy of the medical reports as well, and should begin to compile a file of their own. If the problematic behaviors continue, it's quite likely that more specialists will become involved, as part of a more complex 'behavior analysis.' More evaluations, tests, opinions, and recommendations will likely be added to the mix. The Moffets will need to keep all of this vital information in one safe place, and refer to it whenever necessary.

The next step would be for the special educator to evaluate Jeff for a learning disability. Learning disabilities are usually evident as soon as children start to walk and talk, but many go undetected until the school work becomes more difficult and the child needs to call upon abstract thinking to solve problems. If Jeff hasn't been tested before, now would be the time to rule out a learning disability. A learning disability doesn't always result in the student being an underachiever. On the contrary, we see that many students with learning disability are high academic achievers, some even falling into the genius range. A learning disability is detected by comparing tests that measure Jeff's achievement in language skills and academics with his psychological (IQ tests) and behavior history. In a nutshell, several tests are given to Jeff to assess his academic levels and they are compared to the psychological tests that tell us how *capable* he is of learning. If there is a qualifying degree of disparity between the two, it is concluded that a learning disability exists. For example, if Jeff is capable of learning at a fifth-grade level, but is only achieving at a third-grade level, this is evidence that there is a barrier to his ability to learn (even if he is attending the third grade).

If this is the case, we will then want to look at Jeff's performance tests to determine if there is a discrepancy between the methods he uses to learn. For example, does he retain the information he is given well, or is there a problem with short- or long-term memory? Is Jeff able to score well on individual tasks but unable to see the 'big picture?'

These additional measures should help determine what may be causing him to score lower academically than he is capable of scoring. If Jeff does have a learning disability that had previously gone unnoticed, his frustration around learning may be a factor in his acting-out behavior.

An ADHD questionnaire and behavior assessment should also be administered to Jeff. Once the results of all tests and evaluations conducted thus far are in hand, the professionals involved in the testing should be available for a meeting with Jeff's parents. It may be beneficial to include Jeff in this meeting, but doing so should be well-considered ahead of the meeting, and depend upon whether including Jeff might be perceived as motivating and supportive by him, or simply embarrassing and difficult.

The meeting is a time for team members to report scores, compile their thoughts and ideas, and get input from Jeff's parents. The team should look to Jeff's parents for any information that might be contributing to Jeff's anger and acting-out behavior.

If the team has thus far found no clear reason for the angry acting-out behavior, it's time to turn to a behavior specialist. Depending upon the school district's policies and organizational structure, the behavior specialist might be a school psychologist employed by the school district, the district resource specialist, or it might be a clinician available to the school through the local county mental health program. In any case, the behavior specialist should be trained and experienced in assessing and treating children with behavioral problems. The behavior specialist will compile a great deal of information by collecting the tests administered thus far, interviewing Jeff and family members, as well as teachers, and by observing Jeff in the classroom, on the playground, and possibly in the home environment. Additional psychological tests might also be administered—tests that are more clinical in nature, such as personality tests and projective tests that might bring to light an underlying psychiatric problem not yet identified.

Once fully assessed by the behavior specialist, a comprehensive plan will be put in place. The plan will likely include strategies to be used by the classroom teacher, such as rewarding Jeff, for example, with extra computer time, for short periods of appropriate behavior. Once accomplished, the length of these periods can be gradually expanded. Similar reward systems can be put in place at home. The overall plan will be constantly monitored by the behavior specialist, and modified as necessary.

If an underlying psychiatric problem, such as depression, an anxiety or mood disorder, or ADHD is identified or suspected, the behavior specialist will make an appropriate referral to a physician for a medication evaluation. The physician of choice should be a pediatric neurologist or a pediatrician with a good deal of experience treating children with mental health issues. A child psychiatrist might also be considered.

Additionally, if a mental health disorder is suspected, Jeff and his family should be referred to a mental health clinician with a good deal of experience in treating children, for counseling. Typically, a licensed mental health professional, such as clinical child psychologist, licensed clinical social worker, or marriage and family therapist, is preferable. A psychiatrist should only be considered for providing counseling or psychotherapy if he or she is highly experienced in that particular aspect of treatment. Along with individual therapy for Jeff to address the underlying mental health issues contributing to the angry behavior, Jeff's parents will likely benefit from the support and guidance of a therapist. Just as important, the therapist will likely recommend a series of sessions to include the entire family, where family roles, expectations, and communication can be explored and modified if necessary, to assist in accomplishing goals that are specified ahead of time. For example, Molly Moffet will likely make use of family therapy by opening up about feeling that Jeff takes up most of her parents' attention, leaving little left for her. The therapist might suggest that individual time with Molly be scheduled, even if it's only 30 minutes or 1 hour per week. The Moffets will learn that having the individual quality time to look forward to will go a long way in soothing Molly's unmet need for her parents' attention.

In the rare instances when this stage in treatment has been reached without improvement, it may be necessary for the Moffets, together with the school district, to consider a structured living environment for Jeff, where he will get immediate feedback on his behavior, both positive and negative. In many cases, the school district and county mental health programs can access funding for such group homes, which should be considered only after all other strategies have been exhausted.

The group home for the 'severely emotionally disturbed' child is typically in a residential-type setting, where staff implements a structured 'milieu' consisting of daily group counseling sessions for learning about appropriate behavior, communication, self-esteem, and problem solving. Individual psychotherapy with a licensed mental health professional typically occurs once a week. A 'level system' is typically in place at home, which amounts to each child earning points for advancing to a higher level. With advancements come additional privileges such as outings, availability of video or computer games, and additional free time. Points are generally earned by adhering to rules, interacting appropriately with peers and staff, and completing assigned chores. This type of group home will either operate a 'nonpublic' school on site, or will transport the kids to a nearby public school.

It is our belief that a group home is never an adequate replacement for the loving nurturance of family caregivers, and should be considered only when family-focused services have been exhausted.

It may also be useful for the behavior specialist, prior to recommending out-of-home placement, to consider referring Jeff to a clinic specializing in the latest brain scanning technologies, such as the Amen Clinic. Although still controversial, SPECT scanning to try and identify a neurological basis for behavior problems that have not responded to treatment is showing remarkable results (Amen 2001). Oftentimes, depending on the particular functional abnormality found, specific treatments and/or medications can be recommended for trial.

▶ Managing Your Child's Behavior: The Old and the New

The traditional 'time-out' as a means of managing the angry or defiant preadolescent child's behavior has been used by thousands of parents and teachers for nearly 20 years. The technique, as taught by Dr Thomas Phelan, requires the caregiver to explain to the child in advance, what will happen if the child argues or refuses to do what they are told. When the offense occurs, the caregiver, without emotion or additional discussion, says to the child, 'that's one' and holds up one finger. The child then has the first chance to comply. If the child continues to argue or still refuses to comply, 'that's two,' and two fingers are raised. At this point the child has a second chance to comply. If he still defies the caregiver, 'that's three, take five (or ten or . . .).' Now the time-out is imposed, the number of minutes roughly equivalent to the child's age.

The parent or caregiver might direct the child to their room to serve the time-out, or to a corner of the room the parent expects to remain in for the duration of the time-out.

Once 'sentenced,' the parent/caregiver should not engage in any sort of conversation with the child until their time is completed. If the child is sent to his room for the time-out, any possibility that he might watch television, play video games, play on the computer, or in some other way *enjoy* himself, should be dealt with in advance. The idea is to take the child away from what it is he would prefer to do during the time-out period, in hopes that doing so will cause him to think twice before arguing or breaking the rule in the future.

Essential to the process of a successful time-out is the parent's refusal to get angry or excited, thereby becoming entertainment for the child, or worse yet, reinforcing the child's idea that he can exert power over a *big person* by pushing the right buttons. Letting your child successfully bait you into a power struggle is never a good idea.

But time-out is getting a second look. Forensic psychologist Douglas Ruben (2002) believes traditional time-out may have some usefulness with normally rule-following kids who occasionally misbehave, but that the procedure is widely overused for very noncompliant kids who typically goof-off during time-out, and often manage to sabotage the whole process. An even bigger concern for Ruben is that time-out teaches *interpersonal avoidance*. That is, kids are learning to remove themselves from situations that are conflictual or emotionally uncomfortable, rather than learning to hang in there and draw on their interpersonal skills (the kind of skills taught in this book) necessary to solve interpersonal problems.

Could the result of nearly two decades of time-outs result in husbands and wives, partners, friends, and coworkers heading in opposite directions at the first hint of conflict, irritation, or disagreement? If so, at what price? Walking away is obviously a wise choice when physical aggression might be the next step, but for most of us, with disagreement comes the opportunity for negotiation, compromise, understanding, and enriched interpersonal intimacy. Without working through conflict, what are the chances for love?

Choosing an alternative tool for disciplining an angry child should be done with the particular offense in mind, a practice Ruben refers to as *matching*. In the long run, matching may very well produce more positive results than the one-size-fits-all practice of using time-out for every offense.

▶ Child on Child Anger

Let's take the case of Timmy, who takes an unprovoked slap at Mike. Most often, Timmy is in for a parental tongue-lashing and is sent to his room for a 10- or 20-minute time-out. We'd like to think that Timmy will take the time to reflect on his misdeed, making such an outburst less likely in the future. In reality, the attention bestowed on Timmy, albeit negative attention, may just be exactly what he's looking for. And perhaps more importantly, Timmy has learned a lesson in interpersonal avoidance; to *hit and run*, you might say.

A better approach might be to ignore Timmy's aggressive behavior and Timmy as well, and immediately shower attention and sympathy on Mike. 'Are you okay? What a good job you did to not hit back!' You might place a gentle, comforting hand on Mike's shoulder.

The likely reaction from Timmy will be to make his way to where the action is, looking for some of that good attention. At this point, Ruben contends, the offending child should be ignored for about 15 minutes, a strategy known as the *firewall*, so as not to reinforce the unwanted behavior by giving attention to Timmy. A word of caution here: a likely reaction by Timmy will be, in a sweet and gentle voice, to try and smooth things over, and smooze you, the parent/caregiver or teacher. 'I won't ever do that again. I'll be a good boy from now on.' The parent or teacher who lets Timmy off the hook too quickly ('okay, then,' and all is forgiven) will be teaching Timmy a dangerous lesson: that he can always justify his violence with words, after the fact.

After the critical 15-minute period during which Timmy receives no attention, positive or negative (use common sense here, for example, if your child is having a medical emergency, you'll need to take action), he should be encouraged to make amends to Mike ('say you're sorry'). Once he does so, he should be directed toward a positive behavior ('I'd like you to please pick up your toys and put them in your closet'). Once he's finished, then is the time for Timmy to be complimented up and down, for a job well done.

In *Transforming the Difficult Child* (1998), child therapist Howard Glasser contends that we adults have had it backward since the dawn of man, lighting up like a Christmas tree whenever our child does something we don't like. Glasser suggests that the misbehaving child finds our emotional reaction to be far more entertaining than his favorite toy. We come equipped with all kinds of fascinating bells and whistles: stomping feet, waving arms, red faces, and even a volume control our child can adjust at will. Glasser would like for us to deliver a boring, age-appropriate consequence when our child misbehaves, and to save our unbridled enthusiasm for when our child does something right!

Children can be taught to think differently about anger, and can learn to respond differently to conflict. The tools in the workbook section of this book will be useful to you, in helping your child to do just that. The angry child often lacks the tools necessary to process and express feelings, or to solve conflict without using the maladaptive 'skills' that they have grown *comfortable* with: anger, rage, tantrums, defiance, or all of the above. As unpleasant as these behaviors may be for those of us subjected to them, they are undoubtedly reinforced in some way that makes them 'useful' to the child, and worthy of using again and again. Once *new* skills are learned, practiced, and *reinforced* in a big way, your child is going to see the value of using these newly acquired skills in the future. *Reinforcement is the key.*

Get out of the habit of showering your child with attention when he has behaved in a way that has pushed your buttons. Instead, turn the volume way down on your reaction, make sure he and everyone else involved is safe and protected, and save the bells and whistles for when your child first begins to use the healthier and more pleasant skills presented here.

'Sticks and Stones Will Break My Bones . . .'

'Zero tolerance' has become a twenty-first-century buzz-word. When describing society's unwillingness to accept weapons in schools, domestic violence, child abuse, and gangs in communities, zero tolerance makes terrific sense. But have we possibly taken it a bit too far when we apply zero tolerance to the way people, particularly children, speak to each other?

How does the old saying 'sticks and stones can break my bones but names will never hurt me' fit with a zero-tolerance policy for, say . . . school-yard bullying? Now, we don't suggest turning a deaf ear to the problem of bullying, but do we really want to teach our children that words are truly damaging? Do we want to blur the line between 'hurtful' *words* and physical *violence*? Do we want our kids to conclude that being called a 'geek' on the school playground is roughly equivalent to having their arm broken?

Izzy Kalman (2005) suggests we teach our children to ignore kids who are using words to insult them or make them angry in most cases. 'Though our Constitution guarantees us freedom of speech, we have been teaching our children just the opposite, setting them up for unnecessary conflict' (p. 46).

'He Makes Me so Mad.'

'How does he do that? Does he have a remote control to your brain? Perhaps you're making yourself angry. Besides, even if you decide to let him cause you anger, are you saying that you don't get to decide what to do with that anger? That makes him pretty powerful in your head, right? Something tells me you don't want him to have that power.'

The insulting child is likely looking to feel powerful: like a 'winner,' by making the enemy feel small and defeated. When the offended child reacts with anger, the bully is able to see the fruits of his labor, having had the intended emotional impact over his adversary. A bully will usually become bored in a hurry after firing insults at someone who refuses to respond. *Then* who ends up looking ridiculous? Kalman goes as far as to suggest that the child on the receiving end of the verbal insults respond to the bully as a friend. Let's say Brutus tells Mike he's a stupid loser. Mike could respond in anger, 'Take that back or I'm gonna punch you in the nose.' There's a good chance the bigger Brutus is going to close the distance on Mike, clench his fists, and say something like, 'Oh, yeah? Why don't you *make me* take it back?'

But suppose Mike were to calmly respond to the insult with 'You think I'm stupid? Hmm, I've been working pretty hard to get my grades up. What do you think I should do about it?'

In most cases, Brutus will be at a loss for words. *Then*, who ends up looking like the loser? Not wanting to look like a loser, the bully is most likely going to move on to someone less skilled in dealing with his annoying insults.

We encourage teachers to teach these skills in groups, perhaps to an entire class. The more kids included the better. Once kids see how silly they're going to look if they continue to harass and insult a student that responds as a friend, rather than an enemy, they will think twice before starting the process rolling in the first place. Another huge advantage in presenting these ideas to kids ahead of time is that when kids see this played out, say at recess on the playground, they are going to be struck by the quiet confidence of the student being insulted, and not misinterpret his strategy for weakness. 'Hey, Mike's using what Mrs Kelly taught us! Cool. He's really making Brutus look like a jerk.'

Furthermore, we believe in teaching children that when someone hurts you, it's okay to say so. If we show anger instead, we will get even more anger back. The other person's anger will . . . you guessed it . . . make us more angry! We don't believe this is what you want for your child, in the name of not showing *hurt*.

▶ Harnessing the Power of Humor

Humor is oftentimes nothing more than an insult that is not taken to heart. Think about it. Not responding to insult with anger requires the understanding that we are all imperfect, and the result is *humor*. When this can be done between two people, reciprocally, the result is often *friendship*.

Humor often lies upon that fine line between conflict and peace of mind, and teaching your child to appreciate the value and power of humor is to equip him or her for their life's journey. Being able to laugh at one's self is a critical coping skill in a world where we are taught to take ourselves far too seriously. We doubt that you want your child to walk through life afraid that the words they are about to hear will be damaging to them, and that they therefore need to be in a constant state of physiological arousal and readiness to defend. Instead, model for them the ability to take a lighthearted view of their own imperfections, and those of others, at peace with the knowledge that all humans are imperfect . . . but quite capable of self-improvement.

Life is way too important to be taken seriously.

▶ The Challenge of Energy Management

Reaching your angry child may be especially challenging if he is 'energy challenged,' most apparent in the child diagnosed with ADHD. Glasser and Easley (1998) compare the

ADHD-labeled child to a Cadillac with the brakes of a Model T. All of that powerful forward momentum is not only difficult for you to manage in your child; it is difficult for him to manage in himself. But writing off the ADHD child, or any energy-challenged child, because of an abundance of difficult-to-manage energy is a bit like throwing the baby out with the bath water. Instead, think in terms of shopping for and learning to use a new set of tools, specifically designed to upgrade the breaks of that energetic little Cadillac.

For example, your enthusiastic reaction to the inappropriate social behavior of the overly energetic child will only serve to reinforce the behavior you are trying to extinguish. Instead, be sure that your child understands the rules, and the consequences for breaking them, ahead of time. When the inevitable happens, react in a low-key (boring!) emotional fashion, and provide the previously explained and reasonable consequence. It's important not to confuse 'low-key' with timid or uncertain. You need to show confidence when dealing with your child, leaving no doubt as to who is in charge. This is best accomplished with consistency, and by following through on the consequences (and rewards) laid out in advance. By no means is hollering, hitting, shaking, name-calling, or lighting up like a Christmas tree useful or necessary. A calm and confident display of *taking charge* will convince your child of your conviction in helping him to internalize the necessary energy-management controls (breaks) so essential to his well-being.

Most importantly, from our viewpoint, teach your child to recognize his individual strengths and interests, and show him what can be accomplished when all of that wonderful energy is channeled into those positive activities. Perhaps the strong visual-spatial 'energy challenged' learner who learns to channel that energy into creating with Legos and building model cars and airplanes, seeing the fruits of that energy and noticing your approval for his accomplishments (here is where you may light up like a Christmas tree!), will decide upon a career path as a builder, mechanic, architect, or structural engineer. Perhaps the overly energetic bodily-kinesthetic child who can't sit still to do his homework until he's bounced 300 times on the backyard trampoline or fielded 100 ground rubber balls, ricocheted off of the garage door, will recognize the benefit of burning off that extra energy with physical activity. Perhaps he will make regular exercise a lifelong activity, and along the way, develop the self-esteem of a physically fit and accomplished athlete. Perhaps your musical-rhythmic learner, encouraged to pour that abundance of energy into learning a musical instrument, will gain confidence and self-discipline by making music and entertaining others, and make a healthy habit of expressing and soothing himself with music, throughout a lifetime.

Lastly, the energy-challenged child will require your help in learning the other skills (*executive functions*) necessary to interact in a socially appropriate manner, accurately interpreting the actions of others, confident in identifying and expressing his or her own feelings, planning, being able to self-soothe in healthy ways when necessary, and being able to see the 'big picture.'

The skills taught in this book are just the beginning. Our hope is that you will appreciate their purpose, be energized by their usefulness, and make a habit of applying the same themes and lessons with your child over and over and over again.

▶ Emotional First Aid for the Parent, Teacher, or Counselor of an Angry Child

The 'helper' who is running on empty, is in no shape to reach and teach the angry child. You hear it all the time: 'you better be taking care of yourself or you're going to burn out.' We all know it's true, but are we truly paying attention to the lifestyle choices that will actually make a difference in going the distance with your angry child?

Some basic but important reminders are presented here.

Don't sacrifice rest.

Caring for a child with anger problems can be an exhausting and time-consuming process, but cutting corners on sleep is likely to only make things worse. Sacrificing adequate sleep time can result in irritability, confusion, fatigue, and depression. In some severe cases, psychotic symptoms such as severe paranoia or hallucinations can result. Insufficient rest and sleep can also weaken the immune system, leaving us more susceptible to disease.

Exercise builds stamina.

Exercise can actually rid the body of stress hormones and produce natural pain-killing endorphins, and the increased blood flow that exercise causes is a plus in delivering brain nutrients, and carrying off waste. Exercise is not only good for your body, it's also good for your brain. And who wouldn't welcome the boost of confidence that comes with looking good and being in shape?

Limit caffeine intake.

Counting on a morning boost from caffeine, whether from coffee, soft drinks, or other sources will result in a steep drop-off in energy before lunchtime. Feeling deflated, our inclination is to caffeine-up once again, and the cycle will continue. The more coffee we rely on to keep us going through the day, the more likely we will have trouble getting to sleep at night. Without proper rest, well, see above!

Watch out for alcohol.

Using alcohol to relax in a hurry can be tempting. But having a few drinks can act as a central nervous system depressant, and add to the depressed mood that you might be experiencing as a result of stress. A brain that has become accustomed to relying on alcohol for coping with stress, is likely to be less active, and less healthy overall, than the average brain (Amen, p. 226). The result can be the inability to think clearly, even when not under the influence of alcohol.

Eat the good stuff.

Good fuel for your body is particularly important when you are under stress. Avoid the temptation to make a habit of high-fat, high-sugar 'comfort' foods. Instead, make a habit of colorful foods—green leafy vegetables, berries, beets, and fresh fruit—and be sure to get enough healthy protein in your diet.

Get good fats.

Much of your brain's dry weight is from fat, and fat is essential for your brain to work properly. If your brain doesn't get enough healthy fats, such as the Omega 3 fatty acids contained in fish or fish-oil supplements, it will rely on saturated fats. You've seen saturated fat bubble up from a hamburger patty frying on the stove. A brain relying on this sludge for fat is likely to be sluggish in its operation. If your brain is sluggish, you will be too.

Drink plenty of water.

About 80% of your brain's weight is from water, and without adequately replenishing your body's water supply, your brain won't be operating at its best.

Connect socially.

Being around people that you enjoy is essential for managing stress and feeling content in your life. Just as importantly, it's okay to avoid being with people who bring you down or wear you out. There is no replacement for healthy interpersonal relationships and boundaries.

Care for your soul.

From church to fishing, prayer to yoga, or simply listening to music, you need to nurture your spirit in the ways that make sense to you.

Don't stop learning.

Your brain was designed for learning and learning makes your brain happy. A happy brain makes for a happy person. You are learning at this very moment while reading this book, but learning can come in many forms. Learning that involves music, such as learning an instrument or dance steps, is particularly healthy and rejuvenating. Learning music is thought to work more than one brain system at once.

Plan a strategy with your spouse.

Having cooperation and feeling emotionally supported by your spouse can make a world of difference in your ability to cope. Plan ahead to schedule a break for yourself at a time when your partner can take over for you. A rejuvenating break, doing something you enjoy, doesn't require spending a lot of money. You might take a hike with a buddy, or spend some relaxing time at the local swim center. If you're in a position to splurge, go ahead and pamper yourself. Have a massage or play your favorite golf course. Scheduling the getaway ahead of time gives you something to look forward to, making it easier to hold it together in the mean time.

Be patient with *you*.

Life isn't easy. Raising kids, while probably the most important and fulfilling jobs you can have, is also maybe the most difficult. Like everyone else on the planet, you're still learning. Don't expect perfection.

You might be feeling that you are neglecting those of your kids that don't require as much of your time and energy because of behavior problems. Make a point of spending individual time with all your kids, even if it's just a few minutes a week, reading to each other, playing a game, or talking about their day. Be sure they know they are every bit as important to you as your other kids. Even a few minutes of quality one-on-one time can make more of a difference than you think. You might also involve the other kids in the process of helping the *angry* child. Talk to them about learning styles and let them fill out a survey for themselves. Perhaps they can feel good about using those learning strengths to make a difference in their sibling's growth. 'Jason, you're so good with fixing things. Do you think you might show Justin how to put the chain back on his bicycle? It would do him good to have his bike working to burn off some energy.'

▶ Teacher, Counselor 'Burnout'

Linda is a tutor in an after-school program. She meets regularly with Jason, a 10-year-old fourth-grade special education student. Jason's Individualized Treatment Plan (IEP) is intended to address his behavior problems, which interfere with his ability to learn. He has fallen well below grade level in both reading and math. Jason is often unwilling to follow directions and any attempt to impose consequences results in a rage reaction. Jason has been suspended several times for physically aggressive behavior toward other students and staff. The school psychologist has diagnosed Jason with ODD, and his pediatrician suspects that Jason suffers from the effects of prenatal exposure to alcohol.

Linda tries to meet regularly with Mrs Taylor, Jason's mother, to discuss his progress in the tutoring program. Even though Linda calls to remind her, Mrs Taylor doesn't show up for most scheduled meetings. When she does she is rude, disheveled, and sometimes smells like beer.

Since becoming pregnant, Linda has begun to notice a change in attitude toward both Jason and his mother. She sometimes feels fearful when waiting on Jason to arrive for tutoring. On a recent occasion she told the principal that she was sick when she actually wasn't, and left school before Jason arrived. She has noticed herself feeling angry, even disgusted, toward Jason's mom.

Overall, Linda has noticed feeling more negative about her job. She sometimes calls in sick, even when she's not, and when working with students, Linda sometimes notices that she is less attentive to their needs and often cuts the tutoring short, even when her student seems to be making progress.

Jason is only one of 19 students Linda tutors each week. The majority have behavior problems.

Linda is burning out.

Teachers and counselors who work primarily with children with behavior problems are susceptible to the chronic stress that can lead to *burnout*, a condition defined as 'a syndrome of physical and emotional exhaustion involving the development of negative self-concept, negative job attitudes, and a loss of concern or feelings for clients' (Pines and Maslach 1978, p. 224).

Teachers and counselors experiencing burnout are likely to become cynical about their clients and less supportive than before the burnout developed. The chronic stress condition can result in downplaying the personal accomplishments of the job, a state of emotional exhaustion, and a tendency to no longer see students or clients as individuals. Physical symptoms of burnout may include dizziness, nausea, headaches, fatigue, palpitations, shortness of breath, and cognitive impairment. The majority of subjects studied also experienced symptoms of major depression and panic disorder (Sparks *et al.*, 1990). Substance abuse and difficulty maintaining healthy relationships can also occur.

Teachers and counselors who work with angry kids are frequently exposed to intense emotional arousal. The unpredictability of a sudden, intense, emotional outburst may result in these 'helpers' relying on burnout as a subconscious coping strategy for continuing to do their work over time. To withdraw emotionally, to care less, and to take less personal interest in the individual child may be the mind's way of trying to protect itself from the ongoing stress of the job.

A second factor contributing to burnout for helping and teaching professionals is the sense of not truly making a real difference in the child's life.

A counselor may have the child for only 1 hour per week. While a teacher may have that same child for several hours per day, he is likely one of 20 or more students that the teacher is trying to reach during the same time. A teacher or counselor working as part of a *team* that includes the child's parents and others involved in his care is far more likely to witness the positive results that a team effort can produce, while at the same time feeling the emotional support of the others involved in the child's care.

The simple strategies suggested in the preceding section can go a long way toward preventing burnout, but there are some additional strategies you will want to consider.

In recent years, teachers, especially special educators, have been bombarded with paperwork to meet changing legal requirements in many states. Likewise, counselors and therapists, particularly those dealing with managed care (HMOs), are spending more time on paperwork and less time in direct contact with their clients. A study by Gomez and Michaelis (1995) concluded that less direct contact with consumers in relation to time spent on paperwork leads to reduced feelings of personal accomplishment, a surefire pathway to burnout. It would follow then, that teachers and counselors need to be particularly aware of the first signs of burnout and take appropriate action.

Having some control over one's work environment is one way to lessen the likelihood of burnout. This might be in the form of a flexible work schedule and/or having some control over the workload, having some say-so in what specific services/programs are offered within the school or agency, right down to how your office or classroom is arranged or decorated. Being allowed to apply some personal creativity on the job is essential.

Another factor in minimizing the likelihood of burnout or managing the symptoms is frequent, supportive communication with colleagues. Whether through informal discussion and support in the break room or staff lounge, or more structured, regularly scheduled staff-support meetings, we helping professionals generally benefit from relating to coworkers who often *feel* what we *feel*, when *doing* what we *do*.

Lastly, don't lose sight of the fact that our work is often difficult, and it can sometimes feel that despite our best efforts, we aren't having the kind of positive impact on kids and families that would truly make our work satisfying. To that we say, *take pride and satisfaction in the small successes*. Particularly in times when resources are scarce and paperwork abundant, it may be necessary to recalibrate your expectations and learn to focus on your students' or clients' small successes.

CHAPTER SEVEN

Learning Styles and Why They Matter

Many critics ... believe that, far from slaying the dragon, I have equipped it with additional horns or sharpened teeth. In their pessimistic view, seven intelligences are even worse than one: people can now feel inadequate across a whole ensemble of realms.
— Howard Gardner

Learning strengths differ from person to person. For example, you may have noticed that it is easier for you to learn the basics of gardening by reading through a best seller on the subject, recommended by a trusted nursery operator, than by watching your neighbor as she tends her garden. If so, it's likely you are a strong *verbal-linguistic learner* (learn by reading or listening), and not as strong in the *visual-spatial style* (learning by watching).

On the other hand, perhaps a day watching your neighbor as she tends her garden is just the ticket, in which case, you may be a strong *visual-spatial learner*, or, you may be strong in the *interpersonal style* (and you learn easily by interacting with others). Or maybe the combination of interacting with your neighbor, listening to her explain as she goes, and watching her every move is the perfect comprehensive combination of teaching methods for you (a combination of interpersonal, verbal-linguistic, and visual-spatial learning).

Now let's head to the garage and consider what might have been required for you to learn to work on the family automobile. Maybe you had a difficult time learning about fixing cars by listening to your older brother as he worked, but once you found his shop manual, loaded with diagrams and schematics, you found the tasks much easier to understand. If so, it's a fair bet that you are a strong *visual-spatial* learner. On the other hand, maybe you can study the most highly respected automotive shop manual for hours, and you still can't make heads or tails. Then, by picking up tools and going 'hands-on,' the principles of auto mechanics began to come into focus. If so, you are likely a strong *bodily-kinesthetic* learner (a physical learner who learns best by doing).

There are eight learning styles in all (Gardner 2006).

Some highly respected and fabulously successful individuals throughout history had difficulty learning in ways that others insisted on teaching them. Winston Churchill had difficulty reading and had a speech impediment. He'd fallen so far behind his class that he was placed in the section of the class designated for the 'slow' kids to learn English. Louis Pasteur's father considered him 'stupid' for failing the entrance exam to medical school. The twenty-seventh president of the United States, Woodrow Wilson, wasn't able to learn the letters of the alphabet until he was 9 years old. Albert Einstein actually failed several math classes as a boy and was considered a daydreamer by his teachers. Given his later unequaled ability to conceptualize time and space, what are the chances that Einstein was a

---

SmartHelp for Good 'n' Angry Kids. By Frank Jacobelli and Lynn Ann Watson
© 2009 Blackwell Publishing, ISBN 978-0-470-75802-1

strong visual-spatial learner and was generally bored stiff by the way his math lessons were presented to him?

No matter what their specific learning challenges, the individuals discussed earlier learned to compensate by drawing on their specific individual talents and learning strengths. In *Unlocking Your Child's Learning Potential*, Cheri Fuller writes, 'Your child's learning style is as unique as his or her fingerprint and reflects his or her development, attitudes, strengths and weaknesses. Remember that there is no right or wrong learning style. That is just another way that people are different' (p. 37).

Relying on our individual learning strengths to accomplish tasks is a normal part of our daily lives. By drawing on our individual learning strengths, we are likely to learn and retain more than we would otherwise. We may be strong in one or two styles and not as strong in others. Has your child been given the advantage of learning about feelings, getting along with others, and managing anger, with consideration for his or her *individual* learning strengths? Probably not, until now.

The following will help you to get acquainted with the eight learning styles used in this book for helping your child manage anger.

▶ Overview of the Eight Learning Strengths

The logical-mathematical learner

The child with logical-mathematical intelligence is likely to be a good problem solver, with an interest in numbers, experiments, and puzzles. This learning style first appears when a child begins to show interest in stacking, organizing, or counting toys, or in other ways exploring the world of objects and numbers. David Lazear, author of *Seven Pathways of Learning* (1994), writes that 'logical-mathematical intelligence is responsible for the various patterns of thinking we use in our daily lives, such as making lists, setting priorities, and planning something for the future' (p. 15). The strong logical-mathematical learner might grow up to be a scientist, accountant, computer programmer, or business person.

The bodily-kinesthetic learner

This child has a keen awareness of his body and is likely to display talent in handling objects and controlling body movements. He is likely to enjoy physical activities such as running, dancing, or playing organized sports, and typically prefers to spend time outdoors. This child may be able to soothe himself by going for a run, playacting his emotional dilemmas, or doing jumping jacks. A strong bodily-kinesthetic learner is often good with his hands and may learn best by *doing*. This child may strive to be a professional athlete, mechanic, actor, dancer, or carpenter.

The intrapersonal learner

The strong intrapersonal learner is aware of his inner self. He has the capacity to tell the difference among feelings, name them, and use them as a way of better understanding the ways in which he relates to others, and for managing his behavior. Intrapersonal intelligence involves awareness of inner workings such as thinking processes, intuition, and self-reflection. The child who learns well *intrapersonally* is likely to enjoy spending time alone, learning about feelings, or learning about the inner workings of others. This child may go on to become a counselor or minister, or might choose an occupation in which he frequently spends time alone, such as a long-haul trucker or forest ranger.

The interpersonal learner

This individual has the ability to relate to other people, often having the ability to view the world from another's point of view. The strong *interpersonal* learner is in tune with the moods and temperaments of others, and can often communicate easily, both verbally and nonverbally. Thomas Armstrong, author of *Seven Kinds of Smart* (1993), writes, 'An interpersonally intelligent individual may be very compassionate and socially responsible like Mahatma Gandhi, or manipulative and cunning like Machiavelli.' The interpersonal child will likely show interest in the actions and ideas of others, like reading or hearing stories about others, or show interest in how he is similar or different from others. This child may aspire to be a teacher, politician, therapist, or lawyer.

The musical-rhythmic learner

We use our musical-rhythmic intelligence when we study music or a musical instrument, or when we turn to music to soothe or motivate ourselves. A strong musical-rhythmic learner is likely to appreciate tones, rhymes, and musical beats, and will generally make music and rhythms a common and crucial part of life.

Musical-rhythmic intelligence is often the first to emerge, and is on display when the infant is easily soothed by a mother's lullaby. Gardner (1983) writes, 'During infancy, normal children sing as well as babble: they can emit individual sounds, produce undulating patterns, and even imitate prosodic patterns and tones sung by others with better than random accuracy' (p. 108). The toddler is demonstrating a degree of musical-rhythmic intelligence when showing delight in banging on the kitchen pots with a large wooden spoon.

The visual-spatial learner

The person with high visual-spatial intelligence is very often sensitive to visual detail and can easily memorize what he sees. We show this intelligence when we use a map or read a blueprint. Thomas Armstrong (1993) writes, 'The spatially intelligent person sees things—whether in the "real" world or in the mind—that others are likely to miss' (p. 45).

The child strong in this learning style is likely to enjoy drawing or painting, appreciating color and form, and can easily orient himself in three-dimensional space. This child is likely to enjoy imagining himself on a great adventure, pretending to be invisible, sketching or coloring, and may grow up to become an architect, photographer, artist, pilot, or mechanical engineer.

The verbal-linguistic learner

This individual is good with words. Perhaps the most highly valued in modern society (possibly the reason the IQ test draws so heavily on verbal ability), we call upon our verbal-linguistic intelligence when we put our thoughts into words or down on paper, write poetry, use metaphors, puns, or analogies. Lazear writes, 'Verbal-linguistic intelligence is involved in storytelling and creating, in all forms of humor that involve such things as plays on words, in the unexpected ending in a joke, and in various funny twists of language' (p. 15).

The verbal-linguistic child is likely to enjoy and be proficient in telling stories, keeping journals, playing word games, or debating about his beliefs. Writers, lawyers, journalists, politicians, and advertising agents are likely to be strong verbal-linguistic learners.

The naturalist learner

This individual has a strong connection with nature. He is likely to enjoy animals, the outdoors, and studying or observing the mysteries of the natural world, and have a keen interest in subjects such as biology, botany, geology, and astronomy. He has *nature smarts*.

The child with strong *natural* intelligence is likely to enjoy exploring the outdoors, searching for bugs, climbing trees, collecting and identifying feathers, and learning about the stars. He is likely to strive to become a veterinarian, park ranger, ecologist, oceanographer, or fisherman.

▶ Learning Strengths and Managing Anger

What's the connection?

Most commonly, we (parents, counselors, and teachers) have gone about the challenging task of teaching kids to manage their anger and behavior in the ways that *we* are most comfortable doing the teaching.

Think about it.

Because society so highly values learners who are verbal-linguistically intelligent, and the educational process relies so heavily on these teaching methods, counselors and teachers most often begin their careers fully equipped to use these same skills to teach and counsel. This means *talking at kids*, and expecting that the information will be easily absorbed, just as they themselves were capable of learning and retaining information.

Parents, relying on the most often recommended methods of teaching their kids to manage anger, most frequently rely on the verbal-linguistic approach as well—telling their kids what to do, what not to do, and our personal least favorite, *what to feel*.

But what about the kids who don't learn best by being *talked at*? Many of these kids are 'normal,' undiagnosed (unlabeled) kids who happen to be stronger in learning styles other than the verbal-linguistic style. Many others may be labeled ADD or ADHD, oppositional defiant, learning disabled, 'slow,' or just plain angry. If so, it's a pretty safe bet that most of these kids definitely *do not* learn best verbal-linguistically. In many cases, these same kids become overwhelmed by the frustration they feel at not being able to learn in the same ways as other kids. Their self-esteem suffers as they compare their work and grades to those of their peers. The result is often depression, and a tendency to act out their anger. Doing so too often results in the child being 'diagnosed' with a mental health disorder. Is it possible that the root cause of this inappropriately expressed anger is a lack of appreciation for the individual strengths of the child, and the child's lack of skills (the same skills contained in this book) in appropriately expressing this frustration?

Largely because of the research and writings of scholars like Howard Gardner and Thomas Armstrong in the 1980s and 1990s, educators began to pay attention to the individual learning styles and strengths of their students, and to apply lesson plans that were more individualized than in years past. A study conducted at Sanford Middle School in Lee County, Alabama school system, over the 1994/95 and 1995/96 school years tried to determine whether teacher awareness of individual learning styles would improve student test scores. Reading, language, and regular science classroom teachers attended a 2-day workshop on learning styles, while math and social studies teachers did not. The Stanford Achievement Test was given to 120 fifth-graders prior to their teachers attending the workshop, and then to the same students the next year while in the sixth grade. A summary of the results follows (Williams 2007):

	Fifth grade	Sixth grade
*Reading	40th percentile	70th percentile
Math	44th percentile	40th percentile
*Language	50th percentile	71st percentile
*Science	47th percentile	78th percentile
Social Studies	43rd percentile	39th percentile

The counseling field, however, has been even less inclined to recognize individual learning styles in teaching kids about feelings, and for managing anger and behavior. And where was the anger management workbook for kids that took into account their individual learning styles and strengths? Well, we looked high and low and couldn't find it. And so we compiled every *learning style aware* activity we'd ever used in the classroom and counseling office for teaching kids to manage anger. The result is the book you have in front of you at this very moment. We are very pleased that you do.

Our experience has taught us that identifying and using a child's individual learning strengths makes the teaching and counseling of kids far more successful. A child will learn and retain more important information when he is treated and taught as an individual, rather than simply as a member of a teacher's student body or counselor's caseload (Gardner 1983; Armstrong 1993; Lazear 1994). Why stop at teaching only academic subjects with an appreciation for individual learning strengths? Why not utilize these same individual strengths in teaching kids about feelings, relating to others, and for managing anger and behavior?

SmartHelp for Good 'n' Angry Kids is specifically designed to provide kids with specific tools for managing anger, and these tools are created with consideration and appreciation for each child's individual learning style. The workbook activities in this book have proven remarkably effective for the kids we've taught and counseled. We are convinced that you will achieve similar results with your kids.

We'd like to introduce you to a few of our kids in Chapter 8.

◀ CHAPTER EIGHT ▶

Kaytlin, Thomas, Lena, and Manny: A Few of Our Angry Kids

While a lack of learned skills for recognizing, processing, and expressing anger is the primary reason kids deal with anger in unhealthy and destructive ways, it's rarely that simple. If the extent of that anger is powerful enough to get you to shop for this book then it's a pretty safe bet the anger is being fueled in some way. In many cases, the underlying fuel for a child's anger may be related to that child's neurological makeup, for example a dominating 'reptilian brain,' as when a child's brain development has been upset by trauma (as described by Dr Bruce Perry) or when temporal lobe problems, ADHD, or other frontal lobe deficits are present (as described by Dr Daniel Amen and Russel Barkley; see Chapter 2). Most often, however, the fuel that takes a child's anger from 'normal' to problematic can't be directly attributed to a brain problem, and to help the child put out the fire, it may be necessary to get to know him from the inside out.

We would like to introduce you to a few of our kids . . . and what they taught us.

▶ Kaytlin

Frank had been working as a Mental Health Assistant (MHA) on the adolescent unit of a southern California psychiatric hospital for just a few months when 14-year-old Kaytlin was first admitted. She'd come to the locked unit directly from the emergency department, after superficially cutting her wrists with a barely serrated butter knife. The first time Frank laid eyes on her, Kaytlin had her hands stuffed into the pockets of her heavy tanker jacket, eyes fixed on the floor, hugging the cold sand-colored wall, and she was slowly moving in the direction of the nurses' station for her three o'clock medications. Not interested in exchanging introductions, Kaytlin's straight dark shoulder-length hair hung in her face. When Frank spoke, her large brown eyes rose to meet his for a brief second as she passed, never lifting her head.

It was the duty of the MHA to perform a quarter-hour head check, moving about the unit and laying eyes on each patient, making sure they were safe, and initialing next to their name on a form held firmly on a clipboard. After 2 hours, the MHA would pass the clipboard on to a colleague. During her first few days on the unit, Kaytlin said nothing to anyone, and she appeared to be seething. She stayed in her room nearly all the time, and slept as much as she was allowed. Kaytlin's head-check column consistently read: B/R, B/R, B/R (for bedroom).

The psychiatric unit was shaped like a long dumbbell, a long hallway with the unit entrance intersecting midway. At either end were semicircles of patient rooms, surrounding a 'pod.' The circular pods consisted of a seating area with a table at the very center. Willing patients were encouraged to socialize in the pods when no therapeutic activities were scheduled. The adult patient rooms and pod were at one end of the unit (one weight portion of the dumbbell)

SmartHelp for Good 'n' Angry Kids. By Frank Jacobelli and Lynn Ann Watson
© 2009 Blackwell Publishing, ISBN 978-0-470-75802-1

and the adolescent rooms and pod made up the opposite end. The nurses' station was at the center of the hallway, opposite the entrance. Patients were called via intercom to the station window for medications at scheduled intervals.

Several of the psychiatric nurses and MHAs, including Frank, tried to make inroads in gaining Kaytlin's trust with little or no success. She was determined to 'hideout' geographically, but more importantly . . . emotionally. Kaytlin's need for isolation looked to be something other than shyness or difficulty adjusting to her hospitalization. It appeared she feared her rage might overtake her at any moment, and that she would be unable to contain the damage.

Within a few days of Kaytlin's admission to the program, the unit was rocked by an episode of violence. A young man had come to the unit to visit his girlfriend. Suddenly, he was on his feet exchanging blows and kicks with a male patient, whom the girlfriend had befriended. Apparently overcome by jealousy, and desperately in need of some anger management skills himself, the man was quickly out of control. Fortunately, the male charge nurse on duty that evening was very fit, quick-witted, experienced in the field, and he just happened to be a black belt in karate. Lance was the first staff to arrive to deal with the fight, and Frank was a quick second. Together, they calmly but assertively herded the enraged visitor toward the exit—locked double doors, each containing a 2 × 2-foot shatter-proof glass window.

As the furious young man found himself reluctantly backed up to the doors, the ward clerk inside the nurses' station pushed a button, unlocking the doors with an audible buzzzzz. Still fuming, the visitor yanked on the door handle, making it fly fully open and bang into the wall. As the door swung back toward him, the man punched through the glass, fully extending his arm, then yanking it back through the shredded window. As he retracted his arm, a large shard of glass lodged in his bicep, severing his brachial artery. Suddenly panicking, the man stopped cold and stared at his wound as blood spurted across the hallway, in rhythm with his racing heartbeat. Without quick attention, the man would die of blood loss. Ever the professional, Lance immediately went for a towel to use as a tourniquet, while Frank went for a wheelchair. Within seconds, Lance and Frank rolled the man into the hospital's emergency department, one floor below. The remaining staff rightly agonized over the possibility that observing the terrible trauma would cause a setback in the patients who had seen the events unfold. Kaytlin had been making her way to the nurses' station as the struggle began, and had seen it from start to finish. Interestingly, the event was a turning point for Kaytlin. For reasons that weren't immediately clear, she began to open up in the days that followed. She began moving about the halls without her big jacket. She even began to smile from time to time. What was it about observing the traumatic incident that seemed to make such a difference in Kaytlin?

An hour after the incident, two surgical assistants came to the unit in search of lost tissue from the man's arm that would be essential in trying to save it. The search was unsuccessful, and because of his inability to manage his impulses, he would lose his right arm forever. He did escape with his life, however.

Within days, Kaytlin began looking for attention from Frank, and was willing to talk. She was the youngest of three and the only girl child. Her father was a truck driver and worked long hours. Her mother, who herself was diagnosed with a mood disorder, favored Kaytlin's brothers, and Kaytlin had been the target of her mother's anger for years. Kaytlin stared at the floor while sitting on the edge of her bed, and spoke about the latest incident of abuse that led up to her hospitalization. Her mother had gone ballistic after Kaytlin refused to obey her curfew, heated words were exchanged, and her mother chased Kaytlin around the living room with a lamp in her hand. Finally catching up to Kaytlin, her mother shattered the lamp over Kaytlin's head. The wound to her head was superficial, but the one to her spirit was serious and required hospitalization.

The abuse, both verbal and physical, had escalated dramatically over the previous year, since it had become necessary for Kaytlin's father to take a second job. Her father had tuned out the conflict years before, and refused to intervene on behalf of his daughter. It seemed his way of coping was to be at home as little as possible, and ignore the commotion if he happened to be around when it took place.

The staff concluded that Kaytlin's newfound willingness to open up had likely resulted from observing them deal with the crisis on the unit and she had, on some level, decided she was in a safe place where the adults responsible for her wouldn't look the other way if she were threatened in some way—be it by an outside force or her own destructive rage. Feeling protected, Kaytlin began to talk . . . and talk she did! She quickly developed a reputation for her spontaneous clever articulation, which she frequently punctuated with profanity vulgar enough to make a drunken sailor blush. The internalized rage that had been fueling Kaytlin's depression was finally finding a voice. She repeatedly tested the unit's rules and the patience of the staff. At times, Kaytlin would act out because she couldn't get her way. But most often, her tirades were a result of believing that she, or a peer, had been wronged. Kaytlin's fits of intense rage included yelling at the top of her lungs, slamming doors, even punching of the concrete block walls of the unit. Her knuckles had needed to be X-rayed more than once during her 3-month hospitalization.

Kaytlin's behavior sometimes made it necessary for staff to 'take her down.' A takedown was a maneuver that the unit staff practiced, and amounted to four staff members safely taking patients face down to the floor, to keep them from hurting themselves or someone else. Once the patient was safely contained on the floor, the charge nurse would make a decision on what would happen next. In most cases, the patient would be encouraged to relax while being held to the floor by four big guys. As ironic as that may seem, the patients most often calmed within a few minutes, probably because they now knew they would be kept under control, even if they couldn't do it for themselves. The nurse would then give the go-ahead for the staff to get the patients on their feet and escort them to a seclusion room, a room the kids referred to as the 'Pepto-Bismol' room because of its sickeningly pink walls. Pink was thought to be the most soothing of colors. On other occasions, if the patient was slow to calm down or particularly violent, the nurse would send an MHA for a straitjacket. The jacket would be put on the patients while they were still on the floor. On rare occasions, when the jacket was not enough to gain the patients' cooperation, the staff would hoist them into the air and carry them, head first, to the room.

It might have been a difficult therapy session or a visit from her parents that would set Kaytlin off. At other times, a totally predictable 'no' from a staff member.

Such as in the case of, 'I know it's not snack time but will you let me into the kitchen?'

'No. You'll have to wait for 8:00 snack time.'

Kaytlin could rage over just about anything, and she would give it all she had. Interestingly, she chose never to act out when Frank was working a shift.

'I'd be way too embarrassed to act like that when you're on,' she calmly told him one afternoon.

Hmmm. Kaytlin was acknowledging enough control to decide when she would and wouldn't be out of control. Very interesting.

After arriving on the unit one afternoon, Lance met Frank in the nurses' station and told him that Kaytlin wanted to talk to him.

'She had a tough pass at home. She's in her room.'

After knocking and entering Kaytlin's room, Frank saw Kaytlin laying atop her bed, fully clothed in jeans and a sweatshirt—normal Kaytlin attire. But Kaytlin was in tears.

'I'm sorry,' she managed to whimper. 'I did a stupid thing.'

Frank sat down in the plastic chair next to her bed—its total weight so light as to make a poor weapon or projectile for launching at a window, in hopes of escape. He waited silently.

'I was on pass and I couldn't take my mother ranting at me. I just wanted to die. She had two boxes of over-the-counter sleeping pills in the bathroom cupboard. I took all of it before my dad drove me back here. Nobody knows. I'm sorry,' she repeated. 'Am I going to die?'

Frank had no idea how much of the over-the-counter sleep aid it would take to kill a healthy 14-year-old, but he wasn't taking any chances. He went directly for a wheelchair and brought it back for Kaytlin to climb into.

'I'm sorry,' she said again, the tears still flowing.

'We'll talk about it later,' Frank told her, not wanting his disappointment to show just yet.

Frank rolled Kaytlin up to the nurses' station and went inside for her chart. Lance must have read the urgency on Frank's face. He left the chart he was writing in and met Frank as he approached. A quick explanation and Lance gave the go-ahead for Frank to roll Kaytlin directly to the emergency department. On examining Kaytlin, the emergency room (ER) doctor ordered a dose of Ipecac, a foul-tasting charcoal concoction that would nauseate Kaytlin to the point of vomiting within minutes, ridding her body of any undigested sleeping pills. It worked like a charm, and Kaytlin was none too pleased by the experience. Frank secretly hoped the Ipecac would serve as a 'natural consequence,' an unpleasant event resulting from Kaytlin's poor decision, which might discourage her from making a similar choice in the future. Kaytlin survived the experience.

Months of individual and family therapy followed, and Kaytlin eventually returned home. During treatment, Kaytlin learned from her therapist that the abuse she suffered was not her fault. She and her family began to learn to communicate. Her parents were ordered by the court to attend a parenting class. Her mother was ordered to undergo a psychiatric evaluation and was eventually started on mood-stabilizing medication.

During her final week on the unit, Kaytlin and Frank sat and talked one last time. Curious as to her ability to think into her future, Frank asked what it was Kaytlin saw herself doing 10 years down the line.

'Don't know, really. I know I don't want to have to depend on a man to take care of me.'

Not yet a qualified therapist, Frank passed up the chance to make the obvious interpretation. Her dad had failed to protect her, and so, she couldn't foresee putting any man into that particular position of responsibility in the future.

'It's not a bad idea to have something that no one can ever take away from you. Have you thought about a law degree?'

'Me? A lawyer?' Kaytlin blushed, grinning ear to ear.

'Why not?' Frank went on. 'You're very bright. You get good grades. You care about people, and you are excellent with your words. You can argue like no one I've ever heard!'

Kaytlin chuckled, then went dead serious for a moment.

'I'm gonna have to give that some thought.'

Years later, Kaytlin having tracked down a mailing address, Frank received an invitation to her charter high-school graduation. She was the valedictorian of her class. Three years later came a wedding invitation. And 4 years after that, a law school graduation announcement. Kaytlin went on to eventually become an attorney specializing in intellectual properties and copyright law. She played a role in obtaining a copyright for a book we self-published several years ago for helping kids manage anger.

▶ What We Learned from Kaytlin

At the time she was admitted to the psychiatric unit, Kaytlin was diagnosed with 'major depression with suicidal ideation.' A secondary diagnosis read 'rule out conduct disorder.' Conduct disorder can only be diagnosed in children and teens, and it amounts to a rather severe pattern of violating rules and showing little regard for others (see DSM-IV-TR for the complete diagnostic criteria). A 'rule out' diagnosis is given when the clinician has a suspicion that the diagnosis won't hold water once the patient's issues are more completely understood. Once it became clear that Kaytlin's rebellious behavior was largely a result of the abuse and lack of protection, the rule out conduct disorder diagnosis was dropped.

We learned from Kaytlin, firsthand, how the spirit of a child can be broken by others, particularly those responsible for their basic needs. A parent, teacher, coach, or other responsible adult in a child's life is blessed with the special opportunity to protect and nurture. Failure to do so can damage a child for a lifetime.

We learned that a child experiencing overwhelming emotional pain, and no one to safely confide in, will seek an outlet for his feelings (tossing pebbles from their cup; see Chapter 2). A desperate but common means of expression is through *rage*. Once labeled a 'problem child' with an anger problem, the child's self-esteem continues to decline. When the rage fails as a means for reclaiming a sense of power, self-esteem, or safety, the rage typically becomes internalized, that is, directed inward. The result is, too often, substance abuse, severe depression, even suicide.

How was it possible that no one in Kaytlin's life was willing to point out her strengths? Had it become so important to win the argument or squash her spirit, that no one was willing to take her aside and say, 'the answer is "no," but by the way, you are an amazingly bright young lady with an incredible ability to persuade people to your line of thinking. Have you ever thought about what you might do with your talents?'

Had the adults in Kaytlin's life begun to view her as nothing more than a tool for inappropriately working through their own mish-mash of feelings and issues? Perhaps a more compassionate take on Kaytlin's parents is that her mother had herself been suffering from an untreated mental health disorder, and her father had felt helpless to convince her to get the help she so desperately needed.

Kaytlin's learning strengths were obvious, given her effortless abilities to spontaneously unleash the perfect (if not perfectly *polite*) torrent of descriptive words with which to 'make her case' or defend her friends. Kaytlin was a very strong *verbal-linguistic* learner. Fortunately, in the end, she found a way to recognize her strengths, develop them, and give something special back to the world. Having done so, she was able to view herself in a new and truth-revealing light. A lot of hard work was required of Kaytlin before she was able to see herself clearly and put her life into proper context. Recognizing her learning strengths and putting them to good use made up just a small piece of the hard work necessary. By encouraging Kaytlin to identify and *describe* her feelings, and to talk, talk, talk about her life, she was able to draw upon her strong verbal-linguistic strengths and jump-start the healing process.

▶ Thomas

We first met Thomas when he was 5 years old and participated in the Head Start program. Frank was asked by the program director to observe the children during class time for behavior problems that might require mental health intervention. Rita, the large Native American Head Start director, explained that this was required by the government agency that provides the program's funding. Rita was a kind and patient woman with a very big heart.

During the first classroom visit, Frank observed a cranky and defiant Native American boy who refused to allow any of the other kids to be near him during nap time. While the other kids were winding down and drifting toward sleep, Thomas was lying prone and extending his arms and legs to be sure no one was near. Making contact with another child, Thomas would let out a loud guttural moan, and lash out with his fists and feet. The staff had learned from past experience to walk on egg shells around Thomas, hoping not to provoke him into a full-blown tantrum. Rita watched from a distance, hoping that he would drift off to sleep before his irritation escalated into violence. But Thomas continued to escalate; the once gentle searching motions of his hands and feet quickly becoming punches and kicks.

Frank watched as Rita pondered the situation, and then apprehensively approached Thomas. But rather than confront him on his actions or relocate him, thereby risking a blowup, she moved the several children surrounding Thomas to other positions on the large rubber mat.

What power this little guy commanded in the classroom!

Rita had been concerned about Thomas' behavior for some time, but his mother had apparently made it clear to Rita that he was 'just being a little boy.' She wasn't interested in any kind of help for Thomas. Rita informed Frank that a call to Thomas' mom would only alienate her further. As she had known his mother for several years, she would try once again to convince her that his behavior in the classroom was reason for professional attention.

'I'll let her know that you were here and that you think counseling might help him with his anger.'

A week later, having not heard back from Rita, Frank followed up by phoning her at Head Start.

'She got pretty angry with me,' Rita told Frank. 'She said he doesn't need counseling and wants you to stay out of it.'

A month later, Frank happened to be outside the Head Start classroom on the reservation at the end of the school day. Thomas was standing alone in front of the building. Having never actually had a conversation with Thomas, Frank was surprised to see the big friendly smile on Thomas' face when he approached.

Without even a hello, Thomas began.

'My dad smashed up his car and he might die.'

'I'm really sorry to hear that, Thomas. When did this happen?'

'Yesterday,' Thomas said, still smiling. 'He was drunk.'

Frank was struck by how alone the little boy seemed, and how eager to tell his story. His big, vulnerable smile only added to the sadness of the situation.

And then Thomas walked away in the direction of his home.

The only mental health clinician in a very small and isolated county, Frank had to be constantly aware of how the mental health program was perceived by the community. To be aggressive would be perceived as being overly intrusive, and the residents of a small town value their privacy.

Do I phone Thomas' mom myself? Frank asked himself, staring after the boy. Would she be more willing to consider help for Thomas, given this latest crisis in his life? Confident that Thomas' mom was well aware of the mental health services available to her son, Frank decided to hold off. He later learned that Thomas' biological father had died of his injuries shortly after the accident. Thomas lived with his mother, stepfather, and two older brothers. His mother was 6 months pregnant.

Thomas entered kindergarten the following semester, and his behavior problems worsened. He quickly developed a reputation for refusing to do what his teacher asked of him, sulking, and then exploding like a bomb. By then, Thomas' behavior and learning problems had qualified him for special education services, and Lynn was now coordinating his individualized education plan (IEP) and regularly meeting with Thomas. Speech therapy had also begun to help Thomas with his verbal processing problems—another contributing factor in Thomas' overwhelming frustration. Thomas' mother continued to refuse to consent for Thomas to receive mental health services, however, and Frank could only observe his behavior in the classroom and make recommendations to Mr Preston, Thomas' kindergarten teacher. Frank and Lynn noticed that Thomas would often be working on an assignment, say, drawing a picture of himself playing his favorite sport. Then, he would glance at another student's drawing and begin to sulk, refusing to continue. On some occasions, he would tear up his paper and put his head down on his desk, obviously feeling his work was inferior to his neighbor's and seeming to feel deeply ashamed.

If Mr Preston were to offer encouragement or, worse yet, ask Thomas to continue to participate, the fuse would be lit! Unwilling to chance it, Mr Preston had begun making a practice of ignoring Thomas' behavior and letting him sulk until such time as he decided on his own to rejoin whatever class activities were in progress by then.

Frank suggested that Mr Preston allow Thomas his own space, where he would be less likely to compare his work to the work of other kids. And a corner of Mr Preston's classroom was designated as Thomas' self-soothing space, where he could go without permission at any time that he felt the need to calm himself. The corner was filled with pillows and books with pictures of Thomas' favorite things. But things only got worse for Thomas, and his tirades increased in frequency from about twice per month to twice per week. Thomas was moved from the regular kindergarten classroom to the special day class, where he would have just one classmate, and a teacher's aide with the time to give him special one-on-one attention.

Unexpectedly, after one of his episodes, Thomas told the principal that, the night before, his mother had pushed his little sister into the refrigerator door, bruising her shoulder. As tragic as this was, it also turned out to be an opportunity for Thomas. The County's Children's Services Department conducted an investigation and filed a petition with the court. Included in the petition was the social worker's request that Thomas' mother and Thomas receive psychological assessments, and comply with any recommended treatment. The Superior Court judge approved the petition. Thomas was finally going to get some mental health care! (His mother was also ordered to an anger management program.)

Frank did the psychosocial assessment on Thomas, getting a complete history and spending hours with the boy, talking, playing, and observing him in a different setting. And Thomas was referred to a clinical psychologist, specializing in kids, for psychological testing. Frank quickly learned that just a few weeks prior, Thomas' stepfather, a man he loved and depended upon, had died after being very intoxicated and passing out in the snow-covered yard of a neighbor's home.

That made two lost fathers for Thomas!

In the initial meeting with Thomas' mom, she made clear that she didn't feel it was right for her to be dragged in to see a therapist. And any questions regarding the death of her husband were flatly ignored. Confused, Frank finally asked if there was some reason she didn't want to tell him about Thomas' stepfather.

'In my Native American culture it's considered disrespectful to speak of the dead for one year.'

Frank wished he'd been more culturally sensitive, and apologized for his ignorance. But the interview continued to go downhill after Frank asked about her use of alcohol or other drugs. Thomas' mom took offense, rattled off a few choice words and stormed out. It was becoming clear that Thomas wasn't the only one in his family with an anger problem.

Had there been anyone in Thomas' life to teach him about feelings and how to deal with them?

Frank began meeting one-on-one with Thomas at his school two times per week. He also spent time in the classroom helping with the behavior plan that would help Mrs Tyler, the special day class teacher, manage Thomas and help him get through the day.

Frank began by trying to build trust with Thomas, but it proved to be a difficult task. Both the men Thomas depended on in his young life had tragically left him. And even before those traumas, he'd had a lot of trouble trusting and managing his feelings. Frank did play therapy with Thomas, giving him age appropriate ways to process his feelings, and relaxation training. Thomas agreed to draw a beautiful picture of a place where he felt truly calm and relaxed. Once completed, Frank sat next to Thomas and asked him to talk about his drawing.

Thomas explained that the large figure he had drawn was his dad (his stepdad, whom Thomas considered to be his father). The smaller figures in the drawing, Thomas explained, were the dogs and cats that he had loved but that had died over the course of his young life. The drawing was of his dad taking care of the animals in heaven. Toward the end of every session over the next few weeks, Thomas and Frank would lay on the floor of the small counseling space at the school, previously a janitor's closet, and practice relaxing. Frank would hold the drawing at arm's length above their heads, where they both could see it, and Frank would talk Thomas through a relaxation exercise that included deep breathing, progressive muscle relaxation, and visual imagery. Thomas enjoyed this part of the session, sometimes dozing off to sleep before it was over. A fairly strong bodily-kinesthetic learner, making positive use of the awareness he had of his body and how it worked, was far easier for Thomas than was verbalizing, using logic, or relating to others.

Talking about his life was a huge stumbling block for Thomas. His difficulty went far beyond the limited vocabulary one would expect in a 7-year-old. Thomas would completely shut down before actually talking about his dad, stepdad, mother, or any of the things he had experienced in his 7 years. To push Thomas beyond his comfort zone was sure to cause him to blow. Frank hoped with more time, Thomas would trust enough to start to talk, and express his feelings. Thomas' mother reluctantly met with Frank weekly. The trust-building process with her was slow but steady.

Lynn designed a special learning program for Thomas, and continued to coordinate his individualized education plan. But despite the efforts of all concerned, Thomas' behavior pattern continued and the explosive episodes occurred with even more frequency than when he was in the regular kindergarten classroom. It had become necessary for Frank, Lynn, or other school staff to physically contain Thomas one or two times per week, to keep him from hurting other kids, staff, or himself. The sheriff's office was called on more than one occasion to assist, or to help bring Thomas back to school after he had gone into a rage and run away from the campus, in the direction of home.

Within weeks of beginning in the special day class, Thomas went into a rage after Mrs Tyler asked that he lift his head from the desk and complete a letter-tracing assignment. Thomas launched a chair in Mrs Tyler's direction, narrowly missing her. Six-months pregnant, Mrs Tyler decided her job wasn't worth risking the safety of her baby, and quit her job the same day. It was then that the District Superintendent suspended Thomas from school, pending a special IEP meeting to include the school psychologist and Thomas' mother. Frank and Lynn were also in attendance. The clinical psychologist's report arrived in time for the IEP meeting. He had concluded that Thomas suffered from ODD and post-traumatic stress disorder, and that ADHD and fetal alcohol effect would need to be ruled out—further evidence that Thomas was a very troubled little boy, possibly in need of more structure and intensive treatment than could be provided to him in our small community.

It was the school psychologist's decision to designate Thomas 'severely emotionally disturbed,' an unflattering label that opened a funding stream for more intensive behavioral treatment. The superintendent asked that Frank and Lynn begin looking for a special group home placement for Thomas—his mother was by now in agreement that things could not continue the way they had been, and agreed to visit some placements with Frank and Lynn before a final decision was made.

We learned, weeks after one such visit, that Thomas had ridden 4 hours in the county car with us and his mother, visited a program, and ridden 4 hours back, after suffering third-degree burns on his stomach the day before. Apparently, his grandfather had been trying to teach him the danger of playing with matches. In doing so, he reportedly put a lit match close to Thomas' shirt to let him experience the heat. The shirt burst into flame. Not wanting to risk getting her father into trouble, Thomas' mother applied something from her medicine cabinet to the wound and said nothing.

Another wound from another well-meaning adult family member. How many more would Thomas have to experience? When would the hurting stop?

A ranch-like, family-operated program was chosen for Thomas. In the country, Thomas and the other kids attended a nonpublic school on site and participated in a level-system behavioral program that was fair, consistent, and provided immediate feedback. While most students graduated and returned home within a year, Thomas rarely progressed beyond level one, often acting out in some violent way, or simply refusing to follow the rules. After a year, the program director asked that we try and locate a different program for Thomas.

Sadly, Thomas unsuccessfully worked his way through three more programs in 4 years, each more highly structured than the one before it, and was expelled from each of them because of his violent temper. Twice during that period, the programs resorted to calling the local sheriff's office because Thomas had seriously assaulted staff. Having heard about the groundbreaking work of Dr Daniel Amen (see Chapter 2) Frank arranged for Thomas to have an evaluation at the Amen Clinic and a SPECT scan of his brain. Maybe there was a brain problem that this new evaluation tool could identify. By this time, Thomas had been tried on a number of medications: antidepressants, Klonopin in case there was a type of seizure disorder contributing to his behavior problems, and Cylert and Ritalin for ADHD. The medications had been tried in different combinations and at different dosages. None had helped in the slightest. The Amen Clinic evaluation was a 3-day process and Thomas managed to get through it. He was returned to his placement, and Frank eagerly awaited the Amen Clinic report and recommendations.

Days later, Frank received a call from a juvenile probation officer in the county where Thomas' group home was located.

'We have your boy here,' he said. 'He bit and punched a staff member in the van on the way to school and the program had him arrested.' The probation officer sounded perplexed. 'Strange thing is, kids are always sorry and crying by the time I see them in the detention hall, but not Thomas. He looked at me stone-faced and told me he'd do it again.'

The court in the distant county managed to transfer the case to the court in our county, the county of Thomas' original home, and a hearing took place. A recently elected judge looked over the paperwork in front of him and decided that Thomas had spent enough time away from family. The court placed Thomas with his paternal grandmother on a reservation in a neighboring state. The court ordered that Thomas receive mental health services available to him there. His grandmother elected to admit Thomas to her tribe's outpatient behavioral health program.

The Amen Clinic report arrived days later, and concluded that Thomas had a 'hot spot'—a region of his left temporal lobe (the brain's anger center) was overactive. The report recommended that Thomas be started on Depakote, a mood-stabilizing medication, the report stated, that had proven useful in kids with this particular problem.

But by now, Frank (and the county's behavioral health program), the local school, Children's Services, even the local court, had lost control of Thomas' case and could no longer make his treatment decisions. Quick to forward the report to tribal services and Thomas' mom, Frank could only hope it would be taken seriously.

It was not.

Within weeks, Thomas was picked up by tribal police. At 13, he had been drinking alcohol to the point of losing consciousness, wandering the reservation, and refusing to follow the curfew his grandmother had set for him. Thomas was completely out of control.

Then under the jurisdiction of the tribal court, Thomas was ordered to a tribal juvenile justice detention program. At the time of writing this book, Thomas is scheduled to return home in 3 months, on his eighteenth birthday—the quality of the entire life ahead of him a concern to many who love and care about him.

The sad case of Thomas was included here to stress to the reader the importance of a safe, consistent, and nurturing environment for the kids we serve. Despite the best efforts and intentions of many, a child can be damaged beyond repair. And all of the care, education, and treatment in the world may amount to nothing more than a Band-aid.

▶ What We Learned from Thomas

The lessons we learned from Thomas were difficult ones. Helpers and educational professionals sometimes have trouble accepting their limitations, and we are no exceptions. We would like to believe that we can help any child in need of our help but, sadly, we learned otherwise. It would be comforting to justify our lack of success by telling ourselves our failure with Thomas was solely because we weren't allowed to work with him earlier in his young life, before his brain developed abnormally, exposed to trauma after horrible trauma. And while we continue to believe the delay in providing mental health services to Thomas and his family was a critical factor in his ongoing behavioral difficulties, we will never be sure. How many Thomases can a helping professional care for over the course of a career, and still do his or her work with a measure of confidence?

Undoubtedly, the pattern of intergenerational poverty and substance abuse that existed in Thomas' family and community played an important factor in the outcome of his care. We learned early in our careers that behavior that might be perfectly acceptable to his mother or parents in a child's home may be unacceptable at school. In a historically oppressed culture, such as was the case with Thomas, a Native American, a child's rebelliousness in the larger, dominant society may be considered by his family to be a sign of strength and character, and a reason to feel proud where few other reasons exist. Once reinforced over a period of years, the child knows no other way to behave. To obey the rules and take direction from the dominant culture can result in the child being labeled a 'school boy' by his same-culture friends—a term that implies that the child has turned his back on his own culture and community.

In intergenerational poverty, the goal is to survive each day. Little thought is given to what might occur in the future. Future orientation is a luxury of the middle and upper classes. To understand the worldview of a client, student, or family that has lived in poverty, as have the generations that have come before them, is a necessary step toward helping. Stop. Listen. To try and drag them over to the middle-class train of thought (say, push them to strive for higher education, a white-collar job with benefits and a retirement plan, and vacations in a tropical climate) is to set them up for failure and further frustration.

What is important to them *today*? How can I help them to accomplish that immediate goal? Perhaps what is important today is completing a form for low-income housing assistance, or perhaps arranging transportation for getting their grandfather to town for his dialysis treatment. By doing so, perhaps your client will be freed up to attend her scheduled meeting with the vocational counselor.

You begin to establish trust by showing that you understand what is important to your client, student, or family *today*, and helping to accomplish that goal.

The parents of a disruptive child living in intergenerational poverty love their children no less than in other social classes. Their hopes for their children, however, are often not the same. Thomas' mother's hopes were that her son and other children might somehow not fall into the same patterns of alcoholic behavior that took the lives of both her husbands. She had hopes that Thomas might not be lured into joining a gang, and die on the streets before his fifteenth birthday. She expected that Thomas would be there for all his extended family—to be an integral part of the system each counted on to make it through the day. To hope for more for her son was to hope against hope. Given the expectations and hopes of a mother living in intergenerational poverty, how critical would it be to seek counseling services for a 7-year-old who refused to follow all the rules laid down by his Head Start teacher? In the scheme of things . . . in the course of life on the reservation . . . there were far more important concerns to occupy one's time and attention.

Even though we were able to determine that Thomas was a good bodily-kinesthetic learner, and we used teaching and counseling techniques that would allow him to draw on those strengths (such as the relaxation training described earlier, and feelings identification based on the signals his body gave him before his anger was out of control), Thomas too often operated from the 'reptilian' portion of his brain, common in children who have suffered abuse and/or other significant traumas. The more highly evolved prefrontal cortex of Thomas' brain (the brain's air-traffic controller) most likely developed in a disorganized manner as a result of the chaos in his young life. Thomas' neurological cards were, no doubt, stacked against him. Even the highly structured milieu of the group homes, often effective in teaching disruptive kids about the consequences of their behavior, made no impact on Thomas. For Thomas, cause and effect continued to be only a vague and unachievable concept.

Deeply affected by Thomas and his sad struggles, we are grateful for the opportunity to pass on the lessons he taught us here.

Lena

Lena was an intelligent, curious child in a financially struggling, young but resourceful family. She had a brother 5 years younger. Lena was usually the 'teacher's pet' in elementary school, strong in the logical-mathematical, naturalist, and interpersonal intelligences (see Chapter 6), and she was extremely athletic. She was put into an accelerated class that was designed just for her and two male classmates, who were also strong in Math and Science. But by the time Lena enrolled in middle school, her world began to change. She became suddenly withdrawn and terrified of speaking up in class.

Active in their small community, Lena's parents pushed her to be involved in activities such as pageants, majorettes, church groups, and extracurricular activities. But because of her shyness and unwillingness to speak in front of people, Lena resented their efforts. Her advanced classes were easy for her, but Lena's teachers mistook her boredom and shyness for a lack of caring. She couldn't help but notice that she was different from the other kids, and Lena was becoming angry.

She began fighting with her mother over her mother's rules about clothing and she resisted being pushed into activities she didn't like. As the conflict escalated, the yelling, screaming, and arguing began to get out of control. A self-employed small business owner, Lena's dad was a hard worker and rarely at home, and her mother had her hands full trying to control Lena's fiery temperament.

Lena was bright and she was determined to start making her own decisions, but her parents were at a loss on how to deal with her. They quickly resorted to overcontrol as a means of trying to do what they considered best for Lena. In response to that control, Lena's anger only intensified. If she were to ask her mother to go to her friend's house or wear a new pair of pants to school and her mother said no, Lena would demand to know why not, and the chaos would begin. Lena would run to her bedroom screaming, slam the door, and cry hysterically, or she would run out of the house and into the nearby forest where she found solitude for calming herself, and she would study nature for hours.

Angry at home and relying on running into the woods to soothe herself, Lena continued to be withdrawn at school, fading into the background. As a result, her teachers barely noticed her and failed to recognize her intelligence or her strong individual learning abilities.

To make matters worse, Lena also had a problem with eating, becoming sick to her stomach after nearly every meal. Numerous doctor visits failed to determine the cause.

Lena grew up not liking herself and it wasn't until adulthood when a friend pushed her into counseling that she began to figure out who she was. Until then, she started college but didn't apply herself. She fled from her parents' home at her first opportunity, moving about as far from her hometown as was geographically possible and still be in her native country. But Lena couldn't run away from herself. She had remained angry with her parents, suffered stomach distress on a regular basis, and she had still not recognized her significant individual strengths.

With behavioral counseling, Lena was eventually successful in recognizing that the coping strategies that she relied upon in childhood, namely, a quick temper and running from conflict, were continuing to cause her problems in her relationships. She was able to learn to soothe herself in far more productive ways, often utilizing her creativity and love of nature, such as with arts and crafts, painting, jewelry-making, hiking, and skiing. A particular favorite therapeutic activity in early adulthood was to jog along the backwoods near her home at dusk, while yelling out about whatever frustrations had occurred during her workday, and at the top of her lungs. Certain no one was within earshot, in case she had to struggle for just the right words, Lena was free to let it out at her own pace. By the time she returned home, she had relieved herself of all tension and readied herself for another day.

▶ What We Learned from Lena

During middle school and beyond, Lena lacked an adult in her life willing to take the time to get to know her. The 'system' hadn't allowed for a way to help her identify her individual learning strengths and interests. Once identified, Lena might have been encouraged to develop related skills, such as in math, science, or visual arts, with an eye toward someday giving back to the world in some meaningful way—a surefire building block for self-esteem in youth, and for eventual fulfillment in adult life.

She needed an opportunity, while still young, to learn good decision-making skills and to learn to appreciate her creative mind. Lena's social withdrawal and the shyness that resulted from a lack of self-esteem should have been a signal that special attention was necessary. Had an IQ test been administered in elementary or middle school, it would have been determined that Lena suffered from a learning disability. Despite being bright (in fact it was determined later in life that Lena's IQ fell into the superior range) there was a 25-point discrepancy between her verbal proficiency and performance scores. A simple questionnaire administered around the time of puberty would have indicated that Lena's visual-spatial and logical-mathematical skills were far superior to her verbal-linguistic abilities. In simple terms, Lena was able to visualize concepts and answers in no time flat, but took forever to put them into words. The result was overwhelming frustration, discouragement, and avoidance of social situations that would cause her embarrassment in conversation. Unaware of what was happening, Lena simply concluded that she wasn't good enough.

Unfortunately, Lena didn't get the help she needed as a child because it wasn't available to her. The educational system, particularly at the time, expected that all kids should learn the same way, and that there were smart kids and kids that were not as smart. The smart ones used their words well and scored high on tests. The not-so-smart kids did neither.

In adulthood, Lena was diagnosed with Celiac Disease, an allergy to wheat, oats, rye, and barley (grains containing gluten), and it was determined that this was the source of her daily stomach aches starting in early childhood. Without the necessary diet restrictions, the illness can lead to the intestine's inability to absorb nutrients, and eventually, malnutrition. While in college, Lena changed her major to English, not only because she loved to write but also as a means of improving her verbal-linguistic abilities.

Now in middle age, Lena is able to look back upon a remarkable career in which she has been able to identify the individual strengths of children who are wonderfully unique. Her current wish is that children be given the opportunity to recognize and build upon their individual strengths, to love themselves, and to eventually contribute to changing the world for the better.

Lena's story is not unlike so many kids, especially during adolescence when anger can be a tool for accomplishing the difficult developmental task of individuation (beginning to separate from parents in order to become who we will eventually become), and for venting the frustration of working through the difficult transition. At the risk of being repetitive, not every angry child is diagnosable with a mental health disorder. Many are desperately in need of the time and attention necessary to introduce them to their individual strengths and talents. Lena is a shining example of one highly talented, creative, and intelligent kid who eventually made it. Lucky Lena!

Lena's story is based upon the life of LA Watson, special educator and coauthor of this book.

▶ Manny

Like so many small school districts throughout the country, the idyllic mountain district in which Frank provided mental health services and Lynn taught was short on office space. Upon arriving in the community, Frank learned that his predecessor had counseled at the school a few hours per week. The space she had used, however, had since been converted to the needed storage space. The school's good-hearted principal did what he could to be accommodating, and a card table and chairs were moved into the janitor's storage closet, among the bottles of floor wax, stacks of toilet paper rolls, and mop basin. No sooner had Frank set up shop upon the closet's concrete floor was he introduced to Manny by the county's Children's Services worker.

Manny was a 9-year-old fourth-grader, who until a few months earlier, had lived on a small cattle ranch. His Latino father had been the ranch foreman. Manny's Native American mother had given birth to his baby brother 9 months earlier. Manny was known for his easy smile, cheerful attitude, and his love of baseball. Three weeks earlier, Manny's mother had been sentenced to 14 years in state prison for killing Manny's baby brother.

Frank soon learned that the death had occurred when Manny's mother had become frustrated while trying to bathe his little brother who despised bathing, crying and flailing throughout. Tragically, his mom had given in to the sudden temptation to hold his head under the bath water. In less than a minute, the child's heart had stopped. Manny had since gone to live in the bustling home of his mother's sister, where several of his younger cousins also lived.

Manny and Frank were able to first get acquainted outside the janitor's closet, tossing a baseball and chatting about nothing particularly important. It seemed Manny never stopped smiling, and Frank was immediately touched by his courage and optimism.

At their second meeting, from across the card table, Frank explained to Manny that he talks with kids who are going through a rough time, and that he tries to help them through.

'How do you do *that*?' Manny asked, still smiling.

'By getting to know them. I'd really like to get to know you.'

Manny's smile began to fade and the tears began to come. Manny began to talk about his mom and his baby brother.

'She hurt my brother and now she's in jail,' he told Frank. 'She's gonna be there till I'm old. I get to see her sometimes.' He began.

Frank listened without speaking for as long as Manny was willing to talk about it. Manny would stop and cry when he needed to, then compose himself and go on. He battled with the different feelings that the tragedy had stirred in him. He loved and hated his mom. He missed his baby brother. His dad had closed himself off from the world and gone away, leaving Manny in the care of his mother's sister. In his aunt's home were several cousins. He felt loved there . . . and safe.

Shortly after beginning treatment with Manny, Frank met with his teacher, principal, schoolyard staff, bus driver, and others who would come in frequent contact with Manny. With his guardian's permission, Frank was able to talk with the school staff about Manny's need for their support and patience. His teacher was encouraged to allow Manny to ask for alone time when he needed it. At those times, Manny would be allowed to go out to the school's track and run, under the distant supervision of the principal or a schoolyard monitor. Running, Manny knew, was important for helping him to relax and regroup when he felt overloaded with grief.

Aware of Manny's great love for baseball, Frank encouraged Manny to use a rubber ball to release his anger during sessions. Manny would look at the outside wall of the janitor's closet and imagine the thing that he was mad at. Then toss the ball with all his might, over and over again. Manny could go on for hours. Frank would talk to him through the tosses.

'Imagine the anger leaving your body with the ball as it leaves your hand.'

Bang! The baseball-size rubber ball would pound the wall with all the velocity a 9-year-old could muster. And Manny's magnificent smile would broaden with each toss. After a while, Manny would lead Frank back inside the closet, ready to talk . . . ready to grieve.

Therapy consisted of helping Manny to come to terms with his sense of helplessness. But helplessness is something a 9-year-old athletic little boy is unwilling, and very possibly unable, to discuss. Frustration, on the other hand, was an approachable topic.

'Tell me what you're frustrated about?' Frank would ask.

Relaxed from tossing the ball, Manny was better able to face his inner feelings.

'I want my family back . . . my brother, and my mother.'

'And if there was a way that you could make that happen, you would do it, wouldn't you, Manny? You'd bring your brother back, and you'd bring your mom home?'

Manny began to cry. Frank waited, letting Manny struggle at releasing his hurt.

'If you could make any wish and have it come true, what would your wish be?'

Manny wiped his eyes and looked into the middle distance, thinking.

'I'd have superpowers. I'd bust my mom out of jail and we'd go away . . . my whole family. My little brother, too.'

Frank let Manny sit with his wish for a few moments, allowing him to experience some momentary hope and control over his situation, even if only imagined.

'That's a wonderful wish. Smart boy that you are, you know there is no way to actually make your wish come true. What do you say we talk about what you CAN do?'

The grieving child, overcome by the helplessness to erase the loss or trauma, is prone to destructive anger and violence. Helping the child to cope with the loss is to help him to recognize the source of his helplessness and frustration. Allowing the child to 'make a wish' is a useful way to help the child to do just that.

The counselor, unable to grant the child's wish, may be successful at helping the child come to terms with his loss, by helping him to achieve the next best thing.

'I don't want any of my little cousins to get hurt like my brother did,' Manny told Frank. 'And I don't want any of their parents to hurt them.'

Manny was beginning to think in terms of 'the next best thing.'

Frank and Manny talked about the best ways for Manny to watch over his cousins, to have the kind of relationships that would make it easy for them to come to him if they were in trouble, being hurt, or about to make a bad decision.

Manny would go on to thrive while in his auntie's care. With adolescence came change, however, too often a catalyst for rekindling unresolved grief, and Manny began to struggle with his anger. He eventually required placement in a special school where individualized intensive treatment would be available.

As an adult, Manny continued to struggle with his anger, and he was arrested on several occasions for domestic violence, his grieving remained incomplete.

▶ What We Learned from Manny

The anger-prone grieving child is experiencing a sense of helplessness that is difficult, if not impossible to express verbally, given the limited vocabulary of the child. There is a greater chance that the child will be able to speak about his frustration, and be willing to 'wish' for what would relieve him of his unexpressed helplessness.

We learned from Manny that one child's life can be ended, by one sudden, deadly, unplanned act, and a second child's life forever altered. The surviving child may never 'accept' the extent of the tragic loss, but may 'acknowledge' the resulting pain and summon the courage to examine it head on, in the form of a 'wish.' Once expressed, the child will need to accept that his wish may never be fulfilled but that, with help, he might go on to accomplish the 'next best thing.'

Even when allowed to properly grieve, the damage done to a child in the form of violence and loss will most likely last a lifetime. Sadly, Manny reminded us that grief-related anger, if not resolved, can lead to 'chronic anger' (Sims and Franklin, 2003), unfocused and always close to the surface. In a workshop we attended in 2008, Darcy Sims presented a vivid description of the boy in a state of fear-based chronic anger. He is brushed by another boy while passing in a crowded school hallway, and decides he's been disrespected. Because of his fear of being 'invisible,' he reacts to the boy who brushed him in a defensive and threatening manner. If he can't get respect, he will trade it in for fear. After threatening the unsuspecting boy, the chronically angry boy will bull his way down the hallway, pushing and shoving as he goes, making others fear him as a means of protecting his emotionally vulnerable self.

We fear that Manny has adopted a similar manner of coping with his losses.

◀ CHAPTER NINE ▶

Before You Begin

The purpose of this final chapter is to help you to get the most out of the SmartHelp activities with your child. Though the materials are easy and fun to use, we've included some brief instructions, and ideas for getting you and your child off on the right foot.

Appendix 1 contains the Learning Strengths Survey, scoring materials, and the Eight Pillars Graph, everything you and your child will need for helping to determine his or her learning strengths and interests.

In the workbooks you will find the 48 anger-managing, 'brain-training,' SmartHelp activities for helping your child 'see the big picture,' learn alternative ways to self-soothe before things get out of control, and for processing and appropriately expressing anger.

The results obtained from the materials in Appendix 1 will determine which category of SmartHelp activities in the workbooks your child will likely benefit most from, depending on his or her favored learning strengths. We encourage you to also consider using the activities that correspond with your child's weaker learning strengths, as a means of helping your child to further develop those learning strengths.

Should you choose to use an activity to help your child process his anger while he is still angry or excited, you may find it particularly useful to have your child 'move' first. Allow him to run, kick a ball around, toss water balloons, jump rope, or do jumping jacks. The physical release will likely make it easier for your child to focus on the activity, and think more clearly about the goal. In some children, however, the physical 'release' may actually intensify or escalate the child's anger. If you find this to be the case with your child, you will need to switch tactics. Consider teaching your child to relax by deep breathing. Slowly, in through the nose and out through the mouth. Make the 'in and out' equal in counts. For example, four counts in and four counts out. Four or five breaths should be enough to help your child begin to relieve some tension. It's important to do the deep breathing along with your child. He will have an easier time relaxing if he is looking into your eyes, as you model the behavior for him. You will both need to be careful not to raise your shoulders as you breathe, as this can create, rather than release tension in the neck.

▶ The Learning Style Survey

The purpose of the 64-question Learning Style Survey is to aid you, the helper (parent, counselor, or teacher) to determine the individual learning strengths and preferences of the child you are teaching to manage anger. Your child will enter a 1, 2, or 3 in response to each question. Entering a '1' means the answer is never, a '2' means sometimes, and '3' is for always. The survey contains questions relating to each of the eight learning styles.

Your child should be allowed to complete the survey whenever possible, but it's perfectly acceptable to assist your child with completing the survey, by reading the questions aloud.

SmartHelp for Good 'n' Angry Kids. By Frank Jacobelli and Lynn Ann Watson
© 2009 Blackwell Publishing, ISBN 978-0-470-75802-1

Younger children or kids with a learning handicap may need your assistance. It's also perfectly fine to clarify the meaning of questions for your child.

The process for learning about learning strengths, and the survey itself, should be presented to the child as a fun and exciting opportunity to discover something new about someone *special*.

▶ Scoring the Learning Survey

Scoring the survey is quick and easy. On the scoring sheet, simply enter your child's numeric answers (1, 2, or 3) for each question, above the corresponding question number on the scoring sheet. Total the values for each of the eight learning styles.

▶ Graphing the Results

Entering the survey scores on the Eight Pillars Graph will provide an attention-getting color representation for your child. We suggest that you encourage your child to color in the totaled values in the corresponding columns (pillars), using color markers or crayons. The more colorful the visual representation, the more interest your child will likely take in the results. Learning about his individual learning strengths and preferences can benefit your child for a lifetime.

We have yet to meet a parent, teacher, or counselor who could pass up the opportunity to complete a survey for themselves. Doing so, as well as coloring in an Eight Pillars Graph is especially useful in comparing your child's results to your own. Discussing the similarities and differences with your child is a great way of demonstrating that learning strengths vary from one individual to another, and that one isn't better than the other, just different. Face it. By now, you'll be way too curious about your own individual learning strengths to keep from completing your own Learning Style Survey and Eight Pillars Graph!

The survey is a compilation of our many years of experience working with children, in combination with the work of leaders in the field, including Howard Gardner, Thomas Lazear, and Thomas Armstrong. We encourage you, the helper, to review their fine work. Titles of relevant books and articles appear in the bibliography section of this book.

▶ The Workbooks

Pairing the survey results with the SmartHelp activities

The completed Learning Style Survey and Eight Pillars Graph will result in an individual child profile, giving the child and the helper insight into the learning strengths and preferences of the individual child—in other words, how the child learns best.

These results can now be paired with activities for learning about feelings and managing anger, contained in the workbooks. For example, if the completed scoring indicates that the child may be a strong *visual-spatial* learner, you may choose to begin with the activities in Workbook F. Should the scoring results indicate that your child's second best learning strength is bodily-kinesthetic, you may also choose to use the activities in Workbook B. You may want to move on to your child's third best strength, and so on, making the most of your child's learning strengths and preferences for learning about feelings and managing anger.

Allowing your child to tackle those activities that correspond with his least best learning strengths, with your help and encouragement, may prove useful for helping your child develop those styles of learning.

▶ Thinking, Feeling, Doing: Equally Important Factors in Managing Anger

Behavior problems don't happen in a vacuum, and are not simply a matter of 'bad' behavior. What we *think* about something often determines what we *feel* about it. What we *feel* very often leads to how we *behave* (what we *do* with those feelings). This delicate *thinking, feeling, doing* interplay, is especially important when the manner in which a child processes and then expresses anger is in need of attention. Therefore, we've divided the SmartHelp anger-managing activities into those that focus on *thinking, feeling*, and *doing*, to best address the three separate factors that contribute to expressing anger and managing behavior.

▶ An Encouraging Word to all Readers

We strongly encourage you, the helper, to develop the topic featured in each activity, in a manner appropriate for your individual child and his specific behavior problems. The activities often call for a discussion between helper (parent, teacher, or counselor) and child. This discussion allows for the theme of the activity to be developed far beyond its original simple and general form.

A positive and caring attitude, active listening, and a healthy dose of patience, are the key helper qualities essential in making the most of the SmartHelp activities with your child. Never underestimate the importance of a quality relationship between helper and child in the learning and healing processes. In *Playful Approaches to Serious Problems* (1997), Freeman, Epston, and Lebovitz write, 'When we stay curious and open, our faith is rewarded by the mutual creativity that is generated in our relationship with children' (p. 12).

If your child has a problem with attention, it might be unrealistic to expect him to stay tuned in to the activities for longer than a few minutes at a time. Consider allowing your child to hold on to a fuzzy pipe cleaner while participating in the activities. The fuzzy feel and flexibility might help your child soothe his restlessness, especially for the strong *bodily-kinesthetic* learner. Letting him rock in a rocking chair or bounce on a trampoline are additional ways of managing your child's need to partially divert his attention, while he still takes part and benefits from the activities.

It might be useful to take a break when your child begins to grow restless. Maybe some physical activity will help him to burn off excess energy, and then come back to the activity when he is better able to focus.

Settling for 'I don't know' from your child, is a setup for failure when using the activities. We encourage you to make 'I don't know' off-limits from the get-go. You will likely know when your child is avoiding answering a question in order to play it safe, truly can't come up with an answer, or if he is avoiding the process entirely. Consider letting your child know ahead of time that you will accept his best guess if he's having trouble thinking of an answer. If he's still at a loss, you might want to come up with three possible answers for your child to choose from. When he does, get excited about his answer, and praise him up one side and down the other for not giving up.

You now have everything you need to make the most of the SmartHelp activities for helping your child process feelings and manage anger! Remember to make the activity time with your child, *quality* time for all.

When beginning the SmartHelp activities with your child, you will notice that the themes include correctly identifying the intentions of others, self-monitoring, self-soothing, thought-stopping, learning to appreciate one's own uniqueness, learning from appropriate role models, learning to cope with stressful situations, and to see oneself *situationally*.

In conclusion, we've added a few examples of using a few of the interventions to help your child deal with specific situations that can lead to problems managing anger.

▶ Me in the Mirror

Seth is a 10-year-old fourth-grader who almost always gets picked last when team captains are choosing team members for football. Even after being picked last, Seth gives it his all during the game. But after going back to class, Seth sometimes pouts about having been picked last. By the time he gets home from school, Seth is almost ready to explode.

Seth's mother notices when he comes through the door and goes straight for his room, slamming his door in the process. She follows after Seth.

'Did you have a tough day at school?'

'I hate school! I'm the worst football player in the world and nobody wants me on their team!' Seth hollers.

After listening to Seth vent some of his frustration, his mother introduces Seth to the intrapersonal **thinking** activity, Me in the Mirror.

After reading through the story about Trent, Seth and his mom give some thought to the things that are truly special about Seth.

'Tell you what,' she says, 'let's take turns. I'll write down the first thing and you write down the second. There are so many cool things about you, this will be super easy.'

Seth's mom writes down 'Seth got the best grade in his class on his science project,' and Seth can't help but smile when he sees what his mom wrote.

Shyly, Seth adds to the list. 'I can run like the wind,' and he hands Me in the Mirror back to his mom, for her to add the next special thing about Seth.

By the time they've filled the page, Seth has forgotten all about being picked last, and he's been reminded of some of the things that make him special.

'Think about keeping Me in the Mirror in your pocket at school,' Seth's mom suggests. 'If you feel sad or angry about being picked last again, you can pull it out and read it, and remember what a very special boy you are.'

▶ Bonnie can Balance

Shawna is a serious 12-year-old sixth-grader who sometimes gets overwhelmed with all of her responsibilities. She always does her best and she sometimes gets angry when she hasn't made time for having fun. One Saturday, after dance competition, Shawna sits down to finish her math problems for Monday, and she breaks into tears.

Hearing her crying from his study, Shawna's dad knocks and goes into his daughter's room.

'You okay, sweetie?' her dad asks.

'This stupid math work,' Shawna shouts through her tears. 'I hate my life!' and Shawna tosses her math book against the wall.

'Maybe you've been pushing a little too hard, honey,' Shawna's dad tells her. 'There's school, dance class, the science club, your paper route. And you work so hard at all of it. Anybody would get fed up with having so many responsibilities, and taking them all so seriously. Ever notice how I head for the golf course every Saturday morning? I have to have some balance and so do you. If I didn't I'd be throwing my papers at work, too. And I don't think my boss would like that!'

Shawna and her dad read through Bonnie Can Balance, a logical-mathematical **doing** activity. Shawna is quick to notice how out of balance her life has been lately—all work and no fun. Together, Shawna and her dad think up some things Shawna can change in her schedule, to cut down on the stress, and leave more time for fun.

'Is it really okay that I take some time off from science club, daddy, and use the time for hanging out with Tina and watching movies?'

Shawna's dad is quick to support Shawna's desire to give herself a break.

'I'll be even more proud of you than ever,' he reassures her.

▶ Don't Blow it

Donnie and his counselor have been working on Don't Blow It, a bodily-kinesthetic **doing** activity, for weeks. At the beginning of the school year, Donnie was getting into trouble for losing his temper and putting his hands on other kids, when he thought they were trying to get ahead of him in line, or being too physical on the playground. Practicing deep-breathing and visual imagery gave Donnie important skills that he was lacking. He was able to stop his anger from escalating, and learn to relax.

Donnie, a good bodily-kinesthetic learner and good with his words, could easily describe his anger signals to his counselor when she first introduced him to Don't Blow It.

'I get this hot feeling in my head, like it caught fire, then I start to shake inside. After a few seconds I can't think anymore. I just have to push somebody right out of my way.'

Donnie's counselor was quick to praise Donnie for being willing to talk about the way his body feels as his anger begins. And good in the visual-spatial style of learning, Donnie was able to think up a place that helped him get into the mood to relax.

Together, Donnie and his counselor practiced relaxing, using Don't Blow It as a guide, before they put it to the test. At each counseling session, his counselor asked Donnie if he'd needed to use what he'd learned since the previous session. One day, Donnie told her that he had. The first couple of times he tried paying attention to his body's anger signals and heading off his anger before he blew it, Donnie did less than perfect. His counselor told Donnie how proud of him she was that he'd tried, and they figured out how he could do it better.

'A soon as my head got hot I started breathing,' Donnie told his counselor, 'but the kid kept yelling things in my face, and before I knew it, I went and pushed him. I guess I blew it again.'

Donnie's counselor had a suggestion. 'I think you had exactly the right idea, Donnie. I'm thinking it might be better though, if you turn and take a few steps away from the person while you start your deep-breathing. Maybe being a little ways away will help you to relax and keep control.'

Donnie agreed, and the next time, he walked away before the boy could make things harder for Donnie. The new twist on Don't Blow It worked like a charm.

WORKBOOK A

Logical-Mathematical

This Thing Called Anger

Time required: 20–30 minutes
Materials required: worksheet, pencil or marker
This is a **thinking** activity.

Some people think they understand about the feeling we call anger, but they really don't. To find out what we know about anger, let's read this paragraph and then try to solve the puzzles in the workbook.

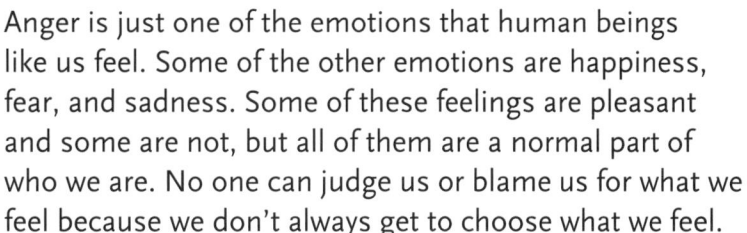

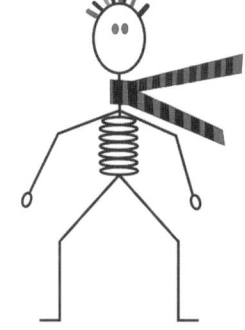

Anger is just one of the emotions that human beings like us feel. Some of the other emotions are happiness, fear, and sadness. Some of these feelings are pleasant and some are not, but all of them are a normal part of who we are. No one can judge us or blame us for what we feel because we don't always get to choose what we feel.

But we are responsible for what we **do** with our feelings. Some things we might do with feelings are healthy and some are not. If we are very sad it is healthy to cry. If we are happy we might smile or laugh. If we are scared we might run away from danger or tell a trusted adult about our fear. If we are angry (same as mad) there are lots of smart and healthy things we can do.

We could tell the person making us mad that we don't like what they are doing, we might walk away from the thing making us mad, we might count to ten, take deep breaths, or ask a trusted adult for help. We might just need to talk to someone about our anger to feel better.

If we use our anger to hurt someone, do dangerous things, break things, or insult others, then we are using our anger in a way that is bad for us and we can expect a consequence we will not like. All of our feelings are special and make us who we are. Our feelings make us notice the things around us and they make life an adventure!

SmartHelp for Good 'n' Angry Kids. By Frank Jacobelli and Lynn Ann Watson
© 2009 Blackwell Publishing, ISBN 978-0-470-75802-1

This Thing Called Anger . . .

Unscramble to answer

                  o r m l a n   t a p r

1. Our feelings are a _____   _____

       f o   w o h   e w   r e a

       __   ___   __   ___

2. Not all feelings are _____ rhymes with

3. When we are feeling mad, which choice will usually get us in trouble?
    a. talk to someone about how we are feeling
    b. ask for help
    c. take deep breaths
    d. push someone
    e. walk away for a few minutes

4. Feelings make life an _____!

Me in the Mirror

Time required: 15 minutes
Materials required: pencil
This is a **thinking** activity.

Trent is an eighth-grader who really loves skateboarding. He practiced every chance he got, at the park, in his driveway; he'd even get up extra early on school days to get on his board. But no matter how much Trent practiced, he could never seem to do the jumps or tricks that some of the other kids could do. Trent started to get really down on himself.

The more Trent struggled the more down on himself he got. After a while, it seemed he couldn't think of one thing he liked about himself. Trent was a very sad and angry eighth-grader, and this made him not so fun to be around!

Well, Trent's mom was worried about him. She could see all the great things about her son that Trent had stopped seeing because he was so disappointed about not being a better skateboarder. So, Trent's mom had an idea. She made a list of all the really cool things about Trent, and showed it to him.

With his mom's help, Trent remembered all kinds of things. These are the ones that made him smile most:

1. Trent is the fastest runner in his class.
2. Trent is a great best friend.
3. Trent gets As in science experiments.
4. Trent has big handsome brown eyes.

Trent was amazed, and pretty happy, to remember that he was a lot more than just a skateboarder. He was the same Trent he'd always been!

Have you looked in the mirror lately? Not the one made of glass, but the one in your heart. What are the really cool things about you? Make a list, draw them, or just have your helper write them for you. (If you get stuck like Trent did, get some help from other people that know you.)

1. _____ 2. _____

3. _____ 4. _____

5. _____ 6. _____

7. _____ 8. _____

Have you looked in the mirror lately?

Draw what you see below . . .

Walt Learns to Wait

Time required: 20 minutes
Materials required: pencil or markers
This is a **feeling** activity.

Walt had a hard time waiting for good things to happen.

If he wanted a new video game he'd ask his mom. If it wasn't in his hands by the end of the day, Walt would be one unhappy boy!

Walt was always getting into trouble for being soooo impatient!

His mom and dad tried to teach Walt that really good things took time. 'When I make your favorite cake,' his mom told him, 'I have to put the flour and the sugar, and the butter all together in exactly the right amounts, then put it in the oven and ... **wait, wait, wait**. If I get in a hurry I get it all wrong, or if I take it from the oven too soon, it just tastes awful!'

His dad told Walt, 'If I get in a hurry when I decide to plant a garden, the vegetables never grow! First, I have to buy the seed, and then turn the soil. Next I have to mix in the fertilizer, and make the rows for watering. Only then can I plant the little seeds. Still, I have to water the garden every day for **weeks,** before I can expect to see anything start to grow!'

Walt wasn't sure he was going to like learning to have to wait, and he realized it would take some **practice**.

Walt and his mom decided to do just that. His mom knew that Walt had outgrown his little bicycle, and he was ready for a new one. She told him that she would pay half, if Walt would earn enough money to pay for the other half. Since Walt was good at doing chores around the house, he decided to start earning money by doing chores for neighbors.

SmartHelp for Good 'n' Angry Kids. By Frank Jacobelli and Lynn Ann Watson
© 2009 Blackwell Publishing, ISBN 978-0-470-75802-1

Walt made a plan and it looked like this:

Wash windows for Mrs Wilson (one time per week for 4 weeks)

Stack wood for Mr Davis (one Saturday)

Wash cars for Mrs Flakus and Mr Abdula (one time per week for 4 weeks)

= one-half the cost of a new bike (in 4 weeks).

Walt realized that it was going to take a whole month before he would be riding his big, beautiful bike, with the cool wind in his face!

But after the month passed, he liked his bike so much that he kept it next to his bed at night! **Waiting and earning his bike, somehow made it even better!**

Together with your helper, think of something you believe is worth waiting for, and make a plan for getting it!

What I WANT

_____

What do I have to do first? _____

Then what? _____

After that? _____

Anything else? _____

Looking at your plan with your helper, how long do you think it will take to get what you want?

_____

Did you know that being able to wait is an important part of growing up? Discuss with your helper.

Figuring Out Who I Am

Time required: 20–30 minutes
Materials required: worksheet, marker or pencil
This is a **feeling** activity.

Figuring out who we really are sometimes takes a little work, and so does solving the puzzle on the next page. It will help if you are pretty good with numbers.

SmartHelp for Good 'n' Angry Kids. By Frank Jacobelli and Lynn Ann Watson
© 2009 Blackwell Publishing, ISBN 978-0-470-75802-1

To find the answer to the question 'WHO AM I?' connect only the dots next to the numbers that are **multiples of the number 3**, that is, if you divide these numbers by 3 you end up with a whole number. Start with the smallest number, then the next biggest, and so on. Good Luck!

```
         2.             8.      36.             42.      48.
    9.   6.     3.              27.  31.  19.
         12.            22.                  80.   86.  85.   4.
   14.          11.       30.   33.      17.       45.
         16.                                            73.  76.
   18.   15.   21.     24.             39.  20.    98.       51.
   61.         64.        208.             131.    7.   34.  55.
                57.       58.          67.         71.            80.
                     54.       69.87.         90.105.     108.
         60.   164.       84.
                          78.          72.   102.      93.  111.       142.
                91.  95.       101.
   136.                   116.         122.       107.      130.  137.
                                151.                    1.
   63.         66.        81.          75.   99.   96.      114.  117.  120*
                               78.
         129.                      203.                209.      92.
   16.                199.                 131.              181.
```

Crack the Cool Code

Time required: 10–40 minutes
Materials required: worksheet, pencil, scratch paper
This is a **doing** activity.

Learning to keep your cool can be a little tricky in the beginning, and this is why sometimes we have to figure out ways to 'keep our cool' by finding out what works best for us. Each of us is an individual and may have different ways of coping with challenges.

So there are a few things you can do before you 'lose your cool' to put your mind in a position to cope with challenges. Next time you are about to lose your cool there is a way to remind yourself to follow a couple of simple steps that will help you get your mind ready to deal with the challenge. First you must **'crack the cool code'** to get the answers.

On the next page, you will have to solve a set of math problems. Once you solve them correctly, you must convert the numbers in your answers to letters, using the **code-cracker decoder**, to find the secret message. **Do you have what it takes to break the code?**

Crack The Cool Code . . .

Even Secret Agents have assistants.

It's okay to ask your helper for help . . .

Secret Agent Cadets:

$$34\,050 + 34\,051$$

$$4\,560\,716 + 4\,560\,716$$

$$1069 - 724$$

$$10\,469\,679 - 2\,358\,332$$

Senior Secret Agents:

$$14\,953\,414 - 14\,885\,313$$

$$1\,140\,179 \times 8$$

$$690 \times \tfrac{1}{2} =$$

$$9\,031\,847 - 920\,500$$

Code-cracker decoder:

```
1  2  3  4  5  6  7  8  9  10 11 12 13 14
P  X  A  N  D  S  K  T  R  O  H  E  I  L
```

Secret Message: __STOP__ __RELAX__ __AND__ __THINK__

Bonnie Can Balance

Time required: 20 minutes
Materials required: pencil or marker
This is a **doing** activity.

Bonnie is a busy girl. Like most kids, school takes up most of her day. Bonnie likes to get good grades so she spends lots of her time doing her homework ... and then there are chores! It's Bonnie's job to feed the cat, take out the trash, and straighten her room ... every day.

But Bonnie can balance! She makes plenty of time for fun, relaxation, and ... well ... just being a kid.

Every day, Bonnie plays for an hour with her best friend Dana, who lives next door. She plays between the time she finishes her homework and the time she goes in for dinner. Bonnie loves soccer and so she plays every Saturday morning. At least once a month, Bonnie has a sleepover with two or three of her girlfriends. They love to listen to music, dance, do each other's hair, and chat about what goes on at school. Bonnie goes for pizza or burgers with her mom and dad.

If Bonnie has too much homework or a test, she may have to change her schedule to make more time for studying. She will add in something that is fun to do the next weekend or find a small reward to give herself after she finishes—like one of mom's cookies. She has learned to be flexible!

SmartHelp for Good 'n' Angry Kids. By Frank Jacobelli and Lynn Ann Watson
© 2009 Blackwell Publishing, ISBN 978-0-470-75802-1

Do you know how to balance?

Use the teeter-totter to name the important things you do because they are your responsibilities, and the things you do just for fun . . .

Responsibilities   **Just For Fun**

_____
_____
_____
_____
_____
_____
_____
_____
_____
_____

Ask your helper for tips.

Remember, happy kids know how to balance!

WORKBOOK B

Bodily-Kinesthetic

Snack-Food for Thought

Time required: 20 minutes
Materials required: markers or pencil
This is a **thinking** activity.

Sarah and Sadie are twins and they love to do everything together.

But Sarah gets sad when Sadie is in trouble, and Sadie gets in trouble a lot! When Sadie's in trouble, Sarah doesn't have Sadie to play with, and she doesn't like that.

One day when Sadie was in her room, taking a long time-out, Sarah got to thinking. 'We're twins, she thought. Why is it that Sadie's in trouble so often and I'm not?'

Sarah remembered something that her teacher had said about what we put into our bodies, and how our body reacts. She remembered that sugar, most of what's in candy and cookies, can make us hyper and nervous, so can caffeine, the stuff that's in most sodas. Full of sugar and caffeine, kids don't make the best decisions.

'Hmmm . . . ' Sarah thought, 'Sadie snacks on a lot of candy and drinks a lot of Sodas and I don't . . . '

When Sadie was done with her time-out, Sarah told her what she had been thinking about. 'I think your snacks are getting you in trouble,' her sister told Sadie. Together they made a snack plan for Sadie.

During snack time at school, instead of cookies and a soda, Sadie would ask her mom to pack: **Crunchy, red apple slices, and a tasty, healthy granola bar!**

After school instead of cookies, Sadie would go for the: **Crunchy, green celery sticks, filled with yummy natural peanut butter!**

SmartHelp for Good 'n' Angry Kids. By Frank Jacobelli and Lynn Ann Watson
© 2009 Blackwell Publishing, ISBN 978-0-470-75802-1

For a nighttime snack, Sadie would ask for: **Cheddar cheese slices on fresh, flaky crackers, and a cold, bottled water!** Before long, Sadie was making better decisions! And Sarah didn't have to play all by herself!

Together with your helper, think about what you've been snacking on. If you've been eating a lot of sugar and caffeine, it's time to make a snack plan like Sadie's.

Make a list of the snack food you have been eating. Then, use the list below it to make your new snack plan! Remember to tell your mom and dad what you've learned about **Snack-Food for Thought**, and ask for their help and permission!

Usual Snack Foods/New Snack-Food for Thought

At School	After School	Before Bed
_____/_____	_____/_____	_____/_____
_____/_____	_____/_____	_____/_____
_____/_____	_____/_____	_____/_____
_____/_____	_____/_____	_____/_____

Good Snack-Food for Thought

Crunchy Apple Slices	A Natural Granola Bar	Cold, Crunchy Pea Pods
Yummy Cheese Slices	A Fresh Cold, Orange	A Cold Glass of Milk
Crunchy Celery Sticks	A Juicy Green Pear	A Pure Glass of Juice
Natural Peanut Butter	A Big, Sweet Banana	Nuts from the Shell

What Are Your Favorite Snack-Foods for Thought?

Frank Feels the Fire

Time required: 20 minutes
Materials required: markers
This is a **thinking** activity.

Feelings are a normal part of life!

Some feelings are very comfortable, like when we feel *happy*. And some feelings aren't so comfortable, like when we feel sad or *angry*.

If we don't pay attention, our anger can get out of control.

Frank was always getting in trouble because he wasn't paying attention to his anger *before* it got out of control, like the time Frank began to get angry when he couldn't get to the next level of his video game. Before long, he got so mad that he threw his controller against the wall, ran into his bedroom and slammed the door. Not only did he have to take a long time-out, but his mom and dad wouldn't let him play video games for a whole month!

Frank's helper taught Frank how to pay attention to his anger before it got out of control. Once he was able to notice it brewing, there were lots of things he could do to keep it from growing.

He could go out for a run, take some deep breaths, phone a friend, or just walk away for a few minutes and try again later. He sure didn't want to lose his video games for a whole month again!

But first, Frank had to figure out where he felt his anger first. His helper told him that some people first feel their anger in their stomachs, and some first feel it in their heads. And some people feel it in their chests. Anger can show up in all kinds of different places.

Frank noticed that sometimes he first felt his anger in his stomach . . . and it felt **like a fire beginning to burn!** Other times he could first feel the fire begin in his head.

SmartHelp for Good 'n' Angry Kids. By Frank Jacobelli and Lynn Ann Watson
© 2009 Blackwell Publishing, ISBN 978-0-470-75802-1

Frank drew himself with the anger just starting, and it looked like this:

Tell your helper about times when you began to get angry.

Where did you feel it?

1. _____

   What happened?

2. _____

   What happened?

3. _____

   What happened?

Can You Feel the Fire Like Frank?

Counting to Calm

Time required: 10–20 minutes
Materials required: worksheet
This is a **feeling** activity.

Bobbie used to get in a lot of trouble for losing his cool. He would not pay attention to his triggers, or his **body signals**, and before you know it . . . he was flying off the handle!

With the help of his dad, Bobbie learned to pay attention to the kind of things that got him angry . . . like when other kids teased him, or when he was having trouble understanding his math work. **Do you know your triggers?** Then, Bobbie learned about his body signals . . . he learned to pay attention to his body when it was trying to tell him he was going to get mad. For Bobbie, his body signals were sweaty palms, a pounding in his chest, and tight muscles in his shoulders. **Do you know your body signals?**

Then Bobbie learned about counting to calm, from his dad. His dad taught Bobbie how to think about something else when he noticed his body was signaling him . . . Bobbie learned about counting to ten.

This was not just ordinary counting. Bobbie learned to picture the numbers in his head each time that he let out a deep breath. Bobbie filled up with air deep down in his belly, then pictured the number '1' as he slowly let the air go. Bobbie would think only about what the number 1 looked like in his head, and his breathing . . . nothing else.

Then Bobbie would fill up with air again and picture the number '2.' He would keep the picture in his mind as he slowly released the air from his lungs. Bobbie realized he was getting more and more calm and in control.

Bobbie repeated this breathing and counting all the way through the number '10,' and when he finished, he noticed that he didn't feel like getting angry anymore.

SmartHelp for Good 'n' Angry Kids. By Frank Jacobelli and Lynn Ann Watson
© 2009 Blackwell Publishing, ISBN 978-0-470-75802-1

List or draw your anger triggers, then discuss it with your helper.

Next, list or draw your body signals, then discuss it with your helper.

And last, draw how you see your calming numbers in your head.

Get help from your helper and practice **Counting to Calm!**

COUNTING TO CALM . . .

With your helper, list or draw your anger triggers:

1. _____
2. _____
3. _____

With your helper, list or draw your body signals:

1. _____
2. _____
3. _____

Draw how you see your calming numbers (1,2,3,4,5,6,7,8,9,10) in your head:

With your helper, practice Counting to Calm!

Rockhound Rhonda

Time required: 15 minutes
Materials required: 'rocks,' shoebox top, paper or cardboard strips, glue sticks, scissors
This is a **feeling** activity.

Rhonda loves collecting rocks and she keeps them in a shoebox under her bed. She looks for all different kinds, colors, and shapes. Some are round and smooth, while others are rough and jaggedy . . . None of Rhonda's rocks are bigger than a tangerine.

Sometimes Rhonda gets confused about how she feels when she's having a tough day. She's not sure if she feels sad, mad, scared, or what . . . her counselor taught Rhonda that it's okay to feel more than one feeling at a time, and she suggested that Rhonda use her great rock collection to help her **get out** her feelings.

Rhonda took her box of rocks with her to see her counselor, and together, they sorted through her collection. Rhonda decided that her very dark and smooth rock would be her **sad** rock, while the reddish pointy one would be her **mad** rock. Her **scared** rock was brownish with dots all over it, and her **confused** rock was all kinds of different colors and it felt very rough on her fingers.

Now Rhonda likes to hold on to a rock while she talks about how she feels. Sometimes when she feels more than one feeling, she holds two or three rocks at once.

By using her rocks, Rhonda was able to get really good at knowing what she is feeling. This makes it way easier for her counselor to help her find ways to feel better!

SmartHelp for Good 'n' Angry Kids. By Frank Jacobelli and Lynn Ann Watson
© 2009 Blackwell Publishing, ISBN 978-0-470-75802-1

Together with your helper, look for the rocks that look and feel like **your** feelings.

After you've collected your rocks, draw a picture of each one below, or place them next to the feeling that best describes them.

My Feeling Rocks

Happy

Sad

Mad

Scared

Confused

Surprised

Now YOU are a ROCKHOUND like Rhonda!

Don't Blow It

Time required: 5–10 minutes
Materials needed: worksheet
This is a **doing** activity.

Deep breathing has been proven to be a very helpful tool for calming down and managing stress. With the help of your helper, you can learn to release the tension your body is holding, every time you exhale. Each time you exhale you can feel more relaxed and more in control.

First, get into a comfortable position. You can close your eyes or leave them open, it doesn't matter. Now, **picture in your mind a place where you have been that was very peaceful**. It might be a place near the ocean or in the mountains, or any place where you felt very calm and relaxed (you can make one up if you want). See it in your mind? Remember that calm feeling?

Next, **put your hand on your stomach and take a deep breath**. Not the way you usually breathe but pull the air deep down into your stomach. Notice how your stomach grows when you breathe in. Now as you breathe out, **imagine that the tension in your muscles leaves your body** along with the air you exhale. Notice yourself feeling more calm and relaxed.

Now breathe normally for a few seconds and, in your mind, **picture your relaxing place**.

Time for another deep breath. Feel your stomach grow ... blow it out ... feel the tension leave your body ... **and picture your relaxing place**. Notice how calm you are becoming?

You and your helper may want to keep this up for a few more minutes, until you are very, very relaxed. Notice how good it feels to be calm and relaxed?

Your helper can teach you to practice breathing to calm yourself until you are so good at it, that you can do it on your own whenever you want. A really good time to practice is when you feel yourself start to get angry.

SmartHelp for Good 'n' Angry Kids. By Frank Jacobelli and Lynn Ann Watson
© 2009 Blackwell Publishing, ISBN 978-0-470-75802-1

DON'T BLOW IT...

Do you know the signals
your body gives you when you are starting
to get angry? Your helper can help you
to learn these signals so that when you feel
them, you can practice your deep breathing.

List the signals here below...

_____

_____

_____   _____

_____   _____

_____   _____

_____   _____

Now draw a picture (or cut a picture from a magazine) of your favorite place, or describe it to your helper and have him/her draw it for you!

Paul Hits the Wall

Time required: 30 minutes
Materials required: ball, wall
This is a **doing** activity.

Paul loves baseball and he loves to play outside for hours!

One of his favorite things to do is toss his baseball-size rubber ball against his garage wall. With every throw, he imagines himself throwing out a runner at first base, or throwing to home plate from centerfield, and keeping the other team from scoring the tying run!

When Paul's had a tough day and feels a little stressed, he takes a few minutes to toss his ball before settling down to tackle his homework.

If Paul is angry because he got his name on the board that day, he will pick a spot on his garage wall, imagine his name on the board, and let the ball fly!

If Paul is angry because the school bully gave him a hard time, he will imagine the bully's face on the garage wall and, you guessed it, let the ball fly!

Paul could **hit the wall** for hours and when he's finished, he feels calm and a little tired in a good way. He just doesn't feel like being angry anymore.

SmartHelp for Good 'n' Angry Kids. By Frank Jacobelli and Lynn Ann Watson
© 2009 Blackwell Publishing, ISBN 978-0-470-75802-1

Draw some garage walls below, and then draw or write down the things that make you angry on them. Maybe it's something that happened today, or maybe something from a long time ago that's still on your mind.

(It's okay to ask for help from your helper.)

Can you look at your garage wall (any wall will do a long as you get permission first) and picture in your mind the things that make you angry?

Let it fly like Paul!

WORKBOOK C

Intrapersonal

Brenda in a Bag

Time required: flexible
Materials required: bag, five special items
This is a **thinking** activity.

Brenda's counselor had a funny way of getting to know her. She asked Brenda to think of five things that tell something about her, put them in a bag, and bring them into the office so that they could look at them together.

Brenda thought of her **Girl Scout pin** because she loved being a Girl Scout, her latest **science quiz** because Brenda wants to be a veterinarian someday, **a letter from her best friend** who moved away last month, **a photo of her grandma and grandpa** whom she loved a lot, and **her puppy, Kiesha's, dog license**. Kiesha died and Brenda loved her very much.

Brenda borrowed a small leather pouch that belonged to her older sister and put her five things inside. Brenda was excited when she brought the pouch into her counselor's office.

One by one, Brenda pulled her things from the bag and told her counselor about each one.

She told her counselor how she earned the Girl Scout pin and why it was extra special to her. Brenda told her counselor the many things that she liked about the Girl Scouts and a few things that she didn't like.

Brenda told about her science quiz and why it was extra special. She talked about wanting to get good grades in science so that she could grow up to be a veterinarian. Her counselor was very interested.

She told about her best friend, Tammy, and how she missed having dinner with her family and spending the night.

Brenda showed her counselor the photo of her grandma and grandpa, and told about the week that she spent with them last summer.

She showed her counselor Kiesha's license and even let her counselor hold it in her hand. Her counselor commented on how smooth and cool the metal

SmartHelp for Good 'n' Angry Kids. By Frank Jacobelli and Lynn Ann Watson
© 2009 Blackwell Publishing, ISBN 978-0-470-75802-1

felt. Brenda explained that Kiesha was the reason that she wanted to become a veterinarian.

Think of five items that tell something special or important about you and share them with your helper! If, for example, you have a horse as a best friend, you might find something that reminds you of him like a blue ribbon or a strand of his long hair. Once you have your five items, share them with your helper.

What will you put in your bag?

_____

_____

_____

_____

Ray on the Rise

Time requires: 20 minutes
Materials required: markers
This is a **thinking** activity.

Ray learned how to use
a thermometer from his school counselor.
It's not the kind that goes under his tongue.
This thermometer is for measuring his cool!

Ray had a tough day that started out when he couldn't find his spelling homework. He looked for so long that he missed the bus! When he told his teacher about his spelling words, she told Ray that he would have to make up the work at recess, and so Ray's best friend gave him a hard time for missing out on football! It was a tough day for Ray, and he could feel his cool slipping away a little at a time, as he got hotter and hotter!

Ray needed a way to figure out what makes him lose his cool and his temperature rise!

Ray and his counselor drew a thermometer like the one below, so that he could get better at noticing his cool slipping away. Once Ray was better at noticing his anger on the rise, he learned some ways to **keep it from getting to boiling!**

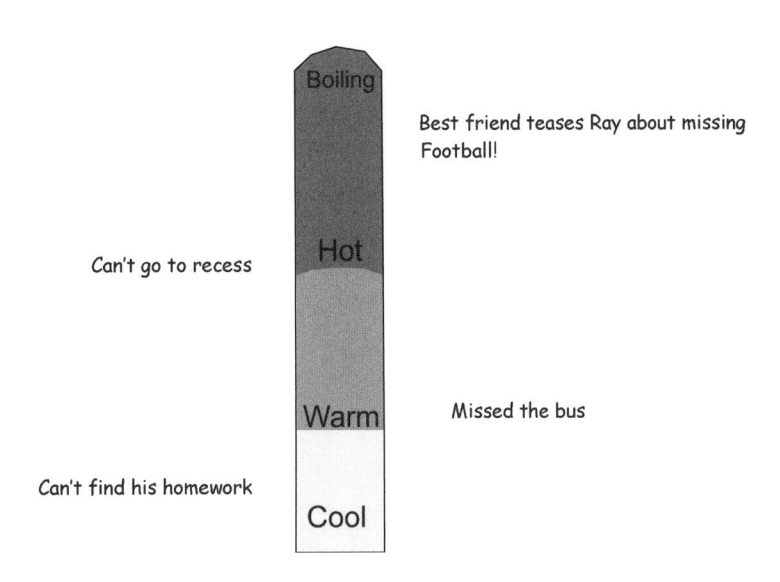

Thermometer:
- Boiling — Best friend teases Ray about missing Football!
- Hot — Can't go to recess
- Warm — Missed the bus
- Cool — Can't find his homework

SmartHelp for Good 'n' Angry Kids. By Frank Jacobelli and Lynn Ann Watson
© 2009 Blackwell Publishing, ISBN 978-0-470-75802-1

Fill in the thermometer below and use it to measure your cool. Label your thermometer with the things that happened to you on a day when you 'lost your cool.'

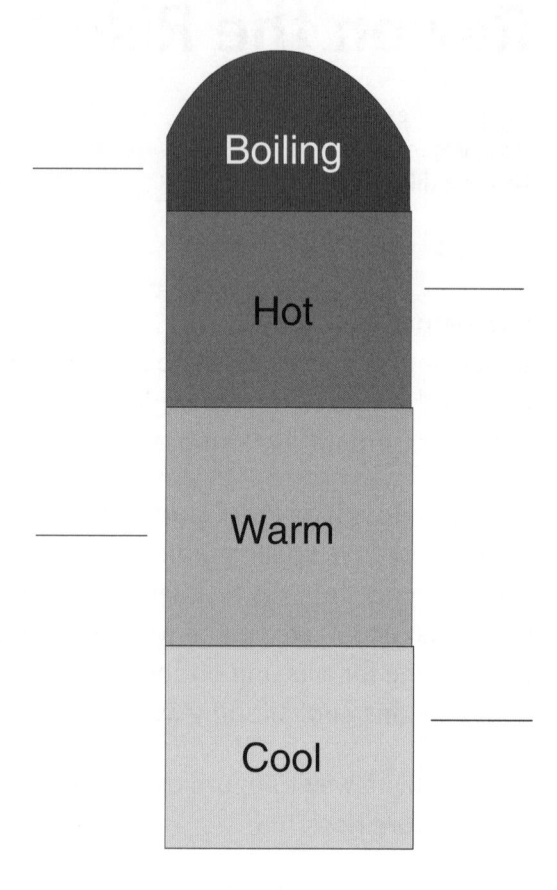

_____ Boiling

Hot _____

_____ Warm

Cool _____

Talk with your helper about the things that make your temperature rise!

My Three Favorite Things

Time required: 20 minutes
Materials required: pencil or markers
This is a **feeling** activity.

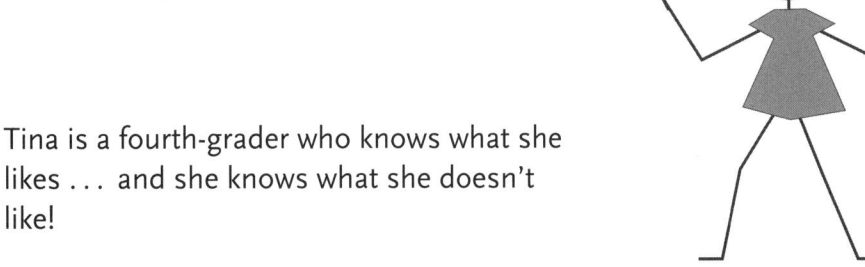

Tina is a fourth-grader who knows what she likes ... and she knows what she doesn't like!

Tina doesn't like to feel **mad, sad, or scared** ... but she knows that uncomfortable feelings are sometimes a part of life.

Together with her helper, Tina figured out how to pay attention to those **three** feelings.

Tina figured out that when she starts to feel **Mad** ... her face feels hot and she makes a fist with both hands!

When she starts to feel **Sad** ... she feels hollow inside and feels a little like crying.

When she starts to feel **Scared** ... she feels a chill pass through her whole body.

Next, Tina and her helper talked about her three favorite things to **do**, when she wants to feel better. They even wrote them down. It looked like this:

Tina's Three Favorite Things

When I feel Mad my favorite thing to do is ... 1. Run like the wind!

When I feel Sad my favorite thing to do is ... 2. Cuddle with my Teddy Bear!

When I feel Scared my favorite thing to do is ... 3. Tell my mom what's on my mind!

SmartHelp for Good 'n' Angry Kids. By Frank Jacobelli and Lynn Ann Watson
© 2009 Blackwell Publishing, ISBN 978-0-470-75802-1

Together with your helper, make a list of what you notice when you feel:

When I feel Mad _____

When I feel Sad _____

When I feel Scared _____

What are your **three favorite things** that you like to do when you have uncomfortable feelings? Write down or draw them here:

When I'm **Mad**

When I'm **Sad**

When I'm **Scared**

It helps to remember your three favorite things!

Color You Calm

Time required: 30 minutes
Materials required: your imagination
This is a **feeling** activity.

Cherie was allergic to peanuts!

She had to be very careful to never eat them. Her family and friends were careful not to bring peanuts around Cherie. But some people like waiters and waitresses, when Cherie went out to eat, sometimes didn't want to take the time to understand.

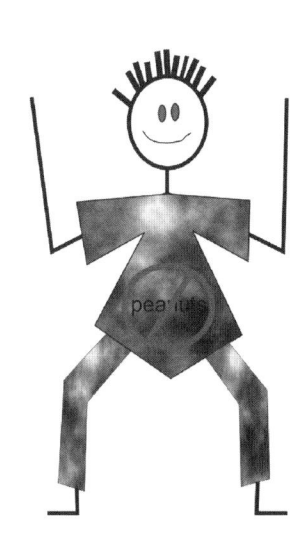

Cherie would get very angry!

Then Cherie remembered a beautiful dream she had, just after she learned about her allergy to peanuts.

She was inside a big balloon as it floated away from earth. As she floated up and up, she became more and more relaxed. Cherie floated through a cloud and bounced around on the heavy fluffy parts. She floated through a rainstorm. The water drops made popping sounds as they bounced off her balloon.

But the favorite part of Cherie's dream was as she floated through a rainbow. Floating up through the colors—Red, Orange, Yellow, Green, Blue, and Purple. As she floated through the Red, she thought about her anger, and then let it go!

The Orange made her begin to feel calm.

Then the Yellow made her relax the muscles in her body.

As Cherie floated through the Green, her mind was clear and very calm, without a worry in the world.

By the time she entered the Blue part of the rainbow, Cherie was feeling very peaceful from head to toe.

When she finally passed through Purple, the last part of the rainbow, Cherie knew she was ready to go home, and she was ready for any problem that came her way! Cherie had learned to relax!

SmartHelp for Good 'n' Angry Kids. By Frank Jacobelli and Lynn Ann Watson
© 2009 Blackwell Publishing, ISBN 978-0-470-75802-1

Draw a picture of YOU in your balloon, floating through the cloud and into a beautiful rainbow!

Together with your helper, get comfortable in your chairs, on a sofa, or on the floor.

Ask your helper to hold your drawing where you both can see it, and imagine floating in your balloon.

Practice moving through the colors: Red, Orange, Yellow, Green, Blue, and Purple.

The more you practice, the easier it will be to Color **YOU** Calm!

When Gary Gets Going

Time required: 30 minutes
Materials required: markers or pencil
This is a **doing** activity.

Gary, an 11-year-old sixth-grader, had a hard time managing his anger! One day in class, Gary's teacher asked for someone to tell her how many continents there are in the world. Gary knew that there are seven and he just couldn't wait to answer! He raised his hand as far as it would go and almost got out of his seat! But when his teacher called on a different student, Gary was so disappointed that he slammed his geography book shut, let out a loud moan, then sat back and folded his arms. Gary's teacher wasn't the least bit happy, and she put his name on the board.

He was getting pretty tired of being in trouble all the time. Gary asked his teacher for some help.

Together, Gary and his teacher were able to figure out ways for Gary to keep his anger under control. They figured out that, before his anger gets out of control, Gary can feel his face get hot and turn red, and he gets kind of a sick feeling in his stomach, like angry butterflies.

Gary told his teacher that he can make himself calm by thinking about his new baby sister and how sweet she smells. And because Gary loves to run and his favorite thing to do is play baseball, Gary can feel good when he looks forward to running the bases at recess. Gary and his teacher practiced switching his thinking to these soothing thoughts whenever he starts to feel his face get hot or the butterflies in his stomach.

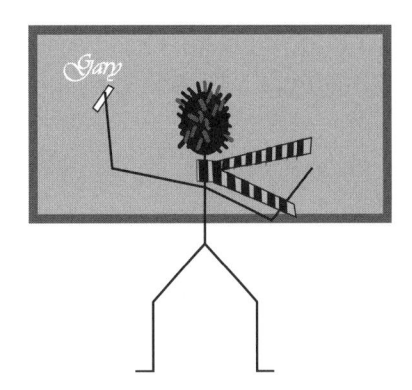

Gary's name on the board

SmartHelp for Good 'n' Angry Kids. By Frank Jacobelli and Lynn Ann Watson
© 2009 Blackwell Publishing, ISBN 978-0-470-75802-1

Gary with his hand in the air

Gary with a red face and butterflies

Gary seeing self running

What do you first notice about yourself when you start to 'get going' like Gary? (Draw yourself)

Together with your helper, choose the thoughts that make you calm.

Like the first drawing of Gary given earlier, think of something that can make you 'get going.' Discuss with your helper what can happen.

Then write down or discuss with your helper what can happen if you switch your thinking to a soothing thought.

```
-------------            -------------
(Me)            (me getting going)            (what can happen)


-------------            -------------
(Me)            (me getting going)            (my soothing thought)
```

Remember to practice switching to your soothing thoughts!

Ben Beats the Blahs

Time required: 20 minutes
Materials required: markers or pencil
This is a **doing** activity.

Ben is a boy who likes to keep busy! When there isn't enough to do, or when he's done the same thing for too long, Ben gets bored. He calls being bored, having the 'Blahs.'

Together with his helper, Ben made a plan for **beating the blahs!**

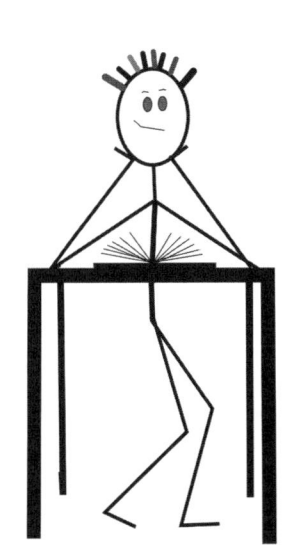

First they made a list of the things Ben likes to do best. It looked like this:

Read a comic book
Play my favorite video game
Practice kicking goals
Play my guitar
Ride my bike

Next, they made a list of times that Ben gets bored. It looked like this:

In the middle of doing homework
When my best friend isn't around
When it's raining outside
When someone else is using the computer
When nothing good is on the TV

Ben and his helper talked about matching up a fun thing to do with the times that caused the blahs. It looked like this:

In the middle of homework ... have 10 minutes to play my video game
When my best friend isn't around ... practice kicking goals
When it's raining outside ... read a comic book
When someone else is using the computer ... play my guitar
When nothing good is on the TV ... ride my bike

SmartHelp for Good 'n' Angry Kids. By Frank Jacobelli and Lynn Ann Watson
© 2009 Blackwell Publishing, ISBN 978-0-470-75802-1

Together with your helper, draw or make a list of the things that you like to do best:

_____   _____

_____   _____

Make a list of times that can give you the blahs:

_____   _____

_____   _____

Now, match the times that can give you the blahs with the things you like to do best:

_____   _____

_____   _____

_____   _____

Use your list to beat the blahs like Ben!

WORKBOOK D

Interpersonal

Sizzling Simon

Time required: 20 minutes
Materials required: pencil or markers
This is a **thinking** activity.

Simon has trouble following the rules!

When he would break a rule, he was punished with time-outs, his best things taken away, and sometimes even spankings. Sometimes there was yelling and crying. But all that punishment didn't seem to help Simon learn about respecting other people or following the rules. Simon would get so mad that his friends started calling him 'Sizzling Simon.'

One day his mom sat down with Simon and said, 'You know, I don't think I've been much help in getting you to follow some very important rules, so I've decided to try a better way to help you.'

Simon was curious. What did his mom have in mind?

'From now on,' his mother told Simon, 'there will be no yelling and crying. I hope there won't be any spankings, or even time-outs. Starting now, I will tell you **exactly what I expect** and if you decide not to follow the rule, you can expect a very "natural" consequence.'

Well, now Simon was very curious. He asked his mom, 'What's a natural consequence?'

'A natural consequence is when someone's behavior just naturally leads to a result they don't like. Say, you leave your bike on the walkway again and I can't get to the front door without moving it. Well, since I'm the one who has to move it, I will decide where I put it. And because I have to move it, I don't have a responsibility to tell you **where** I put it.'

'Or say that you refuse to end your computer time in the computer room, when it's your sister's turn, and your sister begins to complain. What usually happens is you yell back and pretty soon there's a whole lot of yelling and fighting. Well, since it's my responsibility to maintain **order** in the house, the only way I can do that is for you to give up the computer and leave the computer room. Because it's my responsibility, I will give you the option of

SmartHelp for Good 'n' Angry Kids. By Frank Jacobelli and Lynn Ann Watson
© 2009 Blackwell Publishing, ISBN 978-0-470-75802-1

leaving the computer and the computer room, or I will calmly remove you. I will give you the choice of **how** you will leave the computer room.'

Simon was beginning to understand about natural consequences. He was all for not being yelled at or fighting. And he sure didn't like time-outs or spankings. He would give natural consequences a try. He didn't have to be 'Sizzling' Simon any longer!

You and your helper can learn more about natural consequences by using the following activity.

Choose the **natural consequence** you might expect, by circling the best answer:

You leave home without your coat for the third time this week:

a. Your mom will leave her job, drive home for your coat, and bring it to you at school.
b. You will have to take a half-hour time out when you get home.
c. You will be plenty chilly at recess and on the way home from school without your coat.

You leave your football on the porch again, and when you look for it, it's gone:

a. Your dad will run out and get you a new ball before your big game.
b. You can miss the big game because you can't find your favorite ball.
c. You will have to save your money from doing chores, to buy a new ball.

You lose your temper and hit your friend, Billy, while working on your science project

a. You will have to apologize to Billy before he will be your science partner again.
b. You won't be allowed to go to the science fair because you hit Billy.
c. Billy is allowed to hit you back, and no one is going to try and stop him.

Don't Be a Sizzling Simon!

'I,' 'I,' Irene

Time required: 15 minutes
Materials required: marker or pencil
This is a **thinking** activity.

Molly was a lonely second-grader without any friends. Molly lost her friend Suzie after Molly told her '**You** never help me with my spelling words!'

She lost her friend, Amy, when she said, '**You** always beat me to the last swing at recess!'

And she lost her friend Tony when she told him, '**You** made me get in trouble for talking in class!'

Irene is a fifth-grader who noticed Molly sitting all by herself at lunchtime. Molly told Irene how she lost all of her friends.

'I know why,' said I, I, Irene. 'I think "**YOU**" was hurting their feelings!'

Irene taught Molly about using '**I**' instead of 'you,' when she's having a problem with a friend.

Irene said, 'Maybe you could have said to Suzie, "I would really like it if you would help me with my spelling words." Doesn't that sound better?' Irene asked Molly.

'To Amy, maybe you could have said,' "I would like to be able to swing at lunchtime, too."

And to Tony, "I got in trouble because we were talking during class. *I* think we better not do that again."'

Molly said, '**I** get it!' And Molly couldn't wait to start using '**I**' with her friends.

SmartHelp for Good 'n' Angry Kids. By Frank Jacobelli and Lynn Ann Watson
© 2009 Blackwell Publishing, ISBN 978-0-470-75802-1

See if you can change Molly's **YOU** statements into **I** statements, like I, I, Irene:

You broke my bike and now I'm in trouble!

_____

_____

You always get the front seat and I have to sit in the back!

_____

_____

You never come to my house and I always go to yours!

_____

_____

You only play with Sandy at recess!

_____

_____

Can you be like I, I, Irene?

Hannah Asks for Help

Time required: 20 minutes
Materials required: Markers or pencil
This is a **feeling** activity.

Hannah had a hard time asking for help. In school, if she didn't understand what the teacher was explaining, Hannah was too embarrassed to raise her hand. Instead, she would sit and worry . . . and she got further and further behind!

Before long, Hannah was so lost that she would begin to get angry at herself, and after a while, she would blow!

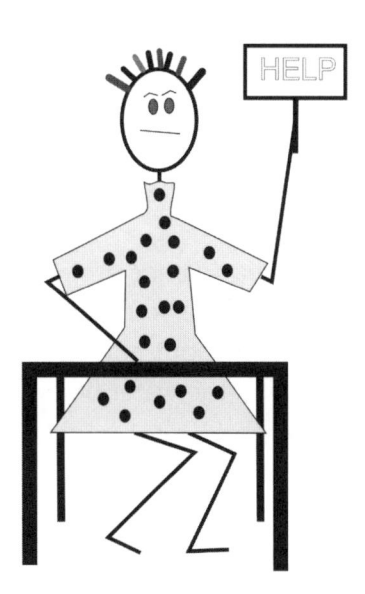

Hannah was afraid to ask for help because she didn't want to look stupid in front of the other kids. But when she would finally get so angry and lose her temper, the other kids stared, and they wondered why Hannah didn't ask for help.

One day at recess, Hannah's teacher asked to talk with her. She told Hannah that not all kids learn the same way, and she would be happy to explain things to Hannah in a way that she would understand.

All Hannah had to do was ask!

Because Hannah wasn't used to asking for help, she wasn't sure how. So her teacher helped Hannah practice asking for help.

SmartHelp for Good 'n' Angry Kids. By Frank Jacobelli and Lynn Ann Watson
© 2009 Blackwell Publishing, ISBN 978-0-470-75802-1

'It's easy,' Hannah's teacher told her. 'And there is more than one way.'

Hannah's teacher told her that she could raise her hand during class and say, **'Mrs Barker, I don't understand.'**

Ms. Barker said that if Hannah didn't understand, there were probably some other kids that didn't understand either, and they would be really glad if Hannah raised her hand.

Mrs. Barker explained that another time to ask for help was at lunch, or recess, or after school, when no one else was around.

Together with your helper, take turns practicing asking for help

Helper: Pretend you are sitting in class while your teacher is explaining a long division problem on the blackboard. But you don't understand what a 'remainder' is. You're a little embarrassed about asking in front of the whole class.

Helper: How would you ask for help?

You are doing a science project with a group of kids who are really good in science (and maybe you're better at art, sports, or spelling). The rest of the group is talking about how heat makes the molecules in water move around, and pretty soon the water boils. But you don't understand what a molecule is.

How would you ask for help?

Helper: You promised your dad that you would rake the leaves in the yard. But it will be dark before you finish and the wind is starting to blow.

Helper: How would you ask for help?

Can You Ask for Help Like Hannah?

Mirroring Matthew

Time required: 20 minutes
Materials required: marker or pencil, a cool friend
This is a **feeling** activity.

Mike used to get mad when other kids got what they wanted. If someone got picked to answer a question, got a better grade, or got a great new video game, he got mad. He was always getting in trouble.

Mike was jealous!

Then Mike made friends with a new boy, Matthew. Matthew was tall and he had a big smile, and everyone wanted to be his friend. Mike was good at football and he taught Matthew how to *bend it*! But Mike learned something from Matthew, too. Mike learned to be happy for other kids!

When Sarah made 100% on the spelling quiz, Matthew told her **'Great Job!'**

When Todd scored the winning goal, Matthew patted him on the back and said, **'Nice shot!'** And Todd was on the other team!

When Nick got the best new video game for improving his grades, Matthew said **'You deserve it. Good for you!'**

Mike noticed that everyone liked Matthew for being kind to other kids, and never jealous. So Mike decided to **Mirror Matthew**.

With your helper, think of some times when other kids got things they wanted.

Using the table below, draw or write down the things that other kids got. Write down what you could say to let them know that you're not jealous.

WHO?	WHAT DID THEY GET?	WHAT COULD I SAY?

Can you be happy for other kids?

Can you Mirror Matthew?

Playing It Cool

Time required: 40–50 minutes
Materials required: worksheet
This is a **doing** activity.

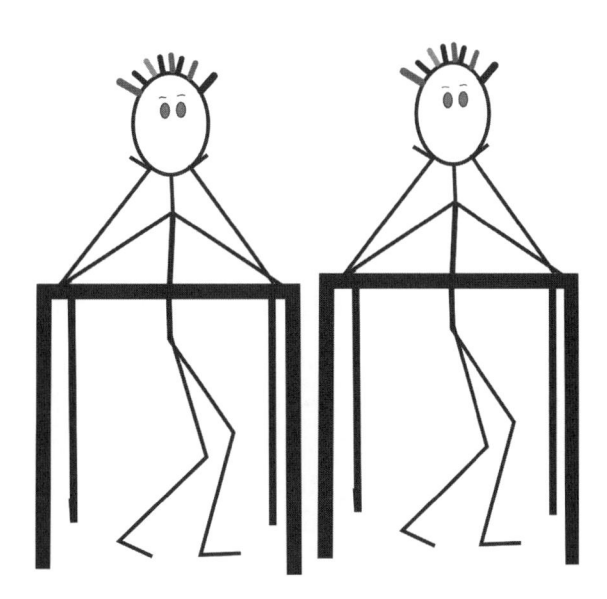

Getting along with others takes practice. Getting through some situations takes more practice than others. Sometimes you have to try to put yourself in another person's place to try to communicate with them. Here is an example:

Tara is very shy in the classroom so she doesn't raise her hand and she acts like she doesn't know any of the answers to the questions the teacher asks. Even when the teacher calls on Tara, she says she doesn't know the answer, even when she does. But Tara gets all As on her tests and report cards.

Susie sits behind Tara and she's always raising her hand even when she doesn't know the answer. She talks a lot and everyone likes her. Susie struggles with her homework and doesn't get it in on time. Her grades are not so good but she is so likeable that her classmates are willing to give her answers to the questions. So Tara and Susie are nothing alike and don't pay much attention to each other. Once in a while, Susie will whisper to her friends that Tara is 'weird' and Tara thinks Susie is a show-off and only thinks about herself. The teacher decides that Susie and Tara could be great partners in Science so he puts them together and what happened was remarkable! They both decided to try to listen to each other and create a final science project together. They began to realize that being different from each other was interesting and important. Susie found out that Tara had the knowledge to create a wonderful project and Tara realized Susie had the personality to

SmartHelp for Good 'n' Angry Kids. By Frank Jacobelli and Lynn Ann Watson
© 2009 Blackwell Publishing, ISBN 978-0-470-75802-1

present the project to others. Tara and Susie created a great partnership using each other's strengths while helping with each of the challenges they faced. They each learned to **play it cool, break no rule, and excel in school!**

Below, there are a few role-play activities that give you a chance to practice three important skills: **asking for help, dealing with an irritating classmate, and apologizing**.

Remember to PLAY IT COOL!

1. Meet Ben. Ben has a hard time understanding his math work. He sometimes gets very frustrated when it seems that he is the only one who doesn't understand. Sometimes he gets so frustrated that he throws up his hands and yells at the teacher, 'Forget this! I'm not doing it!!' **Ben has trouble asking for help**.
   Your helper is going to play the part of Ben and you can play the part of the teacher, when Ben begins to get angry. Notice how your helper is able to pull it together before losing control, by asking for help. Now switch roles and you play Ben.

2. Ted likes to give John a hard time. While on the playground, Ted gives John mean looks, calls him names, and sometimes even pushes him from behind. John gets so angry that he ends up in the principal's office. **John needs to learn how to handle Ted's poor behavior**.
   Your helper will first play John and you play mean Ted. Notice some of the ways your helper deals with Ted's poor behavior. Now switch roles and you play John.

3. Josh's feelings are hurt because his best friend Donnie doesn't pick him for basketball. To get back at Donnie, Josh hides Donnie's backpack for the whole day, and Donnie isn't able to hand in his homework. **After Josh cools down he realizes what he did was wrong but he's having trouble apologizing**.
   Your helper will first play Josh, and you play Donnie. Notice how your helper is finally able to go up to Donnie and apologize. Notice how much better Josh feels. Now switch roles and you play Josh. Saying I'm sorry doesn't have to be hard to do. It just takes a little practice. Being able to apologize helps friends to stay friends for a very long time. After all, everyone makes mistakes!

Chuck Checks It Out

Time required: 15 minutes
Materials required: markers
This is a **doing** activity.

Chuck didn't always understand what people were trying to tell him.

When he got it wrong, sometimes he would get mad, and then get in trouble!

When Chuck's teacher said, 'You missed two questions on your math quiz,' Chuck **thought** she meant, **'This was an easy quiz, you shouldn't have missed two questions,'** and Chuck didn't pay attention for the rest of the day. His parents weren't happy when Chuck's teacher sent a note home!

When his pal, Roger, said, 'I won't be going to your house after school, I have something else to do,' Chuck **thought** he meant, **'I'm not going to your house because I don't want to be your friend anymore.'** Chuck got mad and called Roger a bad name. Then Roger got mad and they nearly got into a fight!

Chuck needed to learn to **Check it Out!**

Together with his helper, Chuck practiced asking the kind of questions that make things easier to understand.

His helper pretended to be Chuck, and Chuck pretended to be his teacher, and then Roger. Chuck's helper showed Chuck how to check it out!

When Chuck said, 'You missed two questions on your math quiz,' his helper asked, **'Is that a pretty good score, or do you think I should have done better?'**

When Chuck said, 'I'm not going to your house after school. I have something else to do,' his helper asked, **'Do you want to come over on a different day?'**

SmartHelp for Good 'n' Angry Kids. By Frank Jacobelli and Lynn Ann Watson
© 2009 Blackwell Publishing, ISBN 978-0-470-75802-1

Read the statements and then circle the best way to check it out!

When your dad tells you he can't make it to your football game on Saturday: (You might think he doesn't want to be at the game.)

a. Do you have something else you have to do, or do you just not want to watch me play?
b. You just don't care about me!

When your classmate tells you he's going to study with Mark instead of you: (You might think he doesn't want to be your friend.)

a. I didn't want to study with you anyway!
b. I was planning to study with you. What happened?

When the new boy beats you in a race: (You might think he wants to make you look bad in front of your friends.)

a. How did you get to be such a fast runner?
b. You're a real jerk!

Talk or draw with your helper about a time when you thought you knew what someone meant, but got it wrong. What happened?

When in Doubt, Check it Out!

WORKBOOK E

Musical-Rhythmic

Larry's Lyrics to Live By

Time required: as long as needed
Materials required: favorite songs, markers or crayons
This is a **thinking** activity.

Larry loves everything about listening to his music. He loves the beat, the sounds of the guitars and drums, and he loves the singers' voices.

He could listen through his headphones for hours!

But what Larry loves most about his music is the lyrics (words).

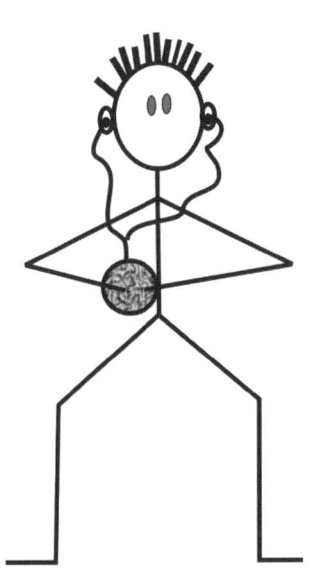

Larry loves the lyrics so much that sometimes he even copies down the words.

The words to his favorite song make Larry think about the things in a new way! If Larry is feeling sad, he will listen to songs that let him feel his sadness, or that **cheer him up**.

If he's feeling angry, Larry will pick a song that makes him feel **calm**, and he'll write down the words.

If Larry is feeling scared or worried about something, he will write down the words to a song that makes him feel **safe and happy**!

After he writes down the lyrics, Larry likes to tape the paper to his bedroom mirror. Just looking at the words can make him feel better about most anything!

If you love music, then the lyrics to your favorite song can make you feel better too!

Write down some of the lyrics of your favorite tunes, and think about how they make you feel.

Name of Song

_____

Lyrics

_____
_____
_____
_____

Name of Song

_____

Lyrics

_____
_____
_____
_____

Name of Song

_____

Lyrics

_____
_____
_____
_____

What are your words to live by? put them where you will see them often!

Rappin' Randy Raps It Out

Time required: as much as you need
Materials required: pencil
This is a **thinking** activity.

Randy loves RAP and HIP HOP music!

He likes to think up words in his head and put them to music. Sometimes he even sings his songs to his friends.

When he was a little boy, Randy would hear a jingle on a TV commercial and it would stay in his head for hours. Finally, instead of trying to get it out of his head, Randy would make up his own words to go with it.

One day while riding the bus home from school, Randy got in trouble for something he didn't do, and he was steaming mad!

Some older kids, sitting behind Randy, were grabbing each other's hats, when a hat came flying over the seat at Randy, and landed in the aisle. Randy went to pick it up and give it back to the boy, and just then, the bus driver looked back to see Randy in the aisle with another boy's hat in his hand.

The bus driver made Randy sit in the front row of the bus for the whole week. Randy told his mom about what had happened, but he just couldn't get it out of his mind. He was being blamed for something that wasn't his fault!

Randy's older sister was getting a little tired of hearing about him so she said to Randy, 'Why not RAP IT OUT!'

'If you RAP OUT your frustrations, there will be more room in your head for GOOD thoughts.'

Randy went to his room with some paper and a pencil, and in no time, Randy came up with this:

(with a RAP beat . . .)

I was sittin' by myself in the back
When my big bros started throwin' hats.
You know I tried to stay clear
but the driver, she looked to the rear.

And there I was with a big ole smile
Pickin' up the hat from the aisle.

Well, you can guess what happened to us
As her words rang through the bus
We heard her loud and clear
'Randy in the rear!
Get your rear up here!'

'And give back that hat'
Then I handed back the hat and sat with my bud, Pat.

So I was pretty mad, 'cus it was me that was had
And now I have a rep for bein' inept.
Tell me how to clear my name
As a kid who plays the hat game!

Think of a time when you were blamed for something you didn't do, and put your thoughts and feeling into song.

Can you RAP IT OUT like Randy?

_____
_____
_____
_____

(Add as many RAP lyrics as you like!)

Bobby Keeps the Beat

Time required: 30 minutes
Materials required: oatmeal box/cardboard box
This is a **feeling** activity.

Bobby was having a hard time keeping his anger from spilling over, and he was pretty tired of going to the principal's office!

One day, Bobby asked the principal if there was someone he could talk to about learning how to calm himself down **before** things got out of control.

Bobby was happy to hear that there was a school counselor that had some great ideas on how to do just that.

At their first meeting, the counselor told Bobby that it was pretty important to pay attention to your body when it's trying to warn you that anger is brewing.

'What do you notice about your body when you first start to get angry?' his counselor asked Bobby.

'It's like there's a hammer pounding in my chest,' Bobby told him. 'My pounding heart gets so loud that I can feel it beating in my ears!'

Bobby learned from his counselor that a lot of people feel their heart pounding when they are getting angry. Bobby was glad to hear that it wasn't just him.

'What good is it to know that my heart pounds when I'm angry?' he asked his counselor.

'Well, if you're paying attention to what your body is telling you, you can do something about it before you're feeling out of control.'

Did you know that before you were born and still in your mummy's body, you counted on hearing the regular beating of her heart? And did you know that when you rock in a chair to relax, you usually rock at the same rhythm as your heartbeat?

Bobby **didn't** know, but he was eager to hear more.

SmartHelp for Good 'n' Angry Kids. By Frank Jacobelli and Lynn Ann Watson
© 2009 Blackwell Publishing, ISBN 978-0-470-75802-1

Bobby learned that we can calm ourselves by getting into our body's natural rhythms, like the normal rhythm of our hearts.

His counselor showed Bobby how to make a drum out of an oatmeal box, and the counselor made one for himself at the same time.

Together, they practiced paying attention to the rhythm of their heartbeats by putting a finger on their pulses for a few seconds, then imitating the same beat on their drums.

Boom **BOOM**, boom **BOOM**, boom **BOOM**, boom **BOOM**, boom **BOOM** . . .

After practicing a few times with his counselor, Bobby was able to go to his room and use his drum, whenever he started to feel his heart pound . . .

At school, Bobby got good at tapping his finger lightly on his desk, at the same rhythm as his normal heartbeat . . .

Make yourself a drum from an oatmeal box, using these step-by-step directions:

1. Take the top and bottom off the box. Cut two circles, an inch wider than the box, out of an old rubber tire tube.
2. Punch small holes every inch or so, around the edges of the rubber circles.
3. Feed a string through the holes in the rubber circles, wrap them around the top and bottom of the box, and tighten until you can hear a beat!

Practice Keeping the Beat like Bobby!

Sam's Secret Saying

Time required: 30 minutes
Materials required: pencil or markers
This is a **feeling** activity.

Sam has a secret saying!

He says his saying to himself whenever he wants to stay cool and not lose his temper.

Before Sam had a secret saying, he would let other kids make him angry. Sam would scream and holler. His face would turn red and his eyes would bulge out, and then he would do things that would get him in lots of trouble.

Sam was sick and tired of being in trouble, and so he asked his teacher for help. After class, Sam's teacher taught him how to not let the other kids get to him.

'You are giving all your power away,' she told him. 'When you let them make you angry, the other kids win.'

Sam asked for help. 'What can I do?' he asked his teacher.

'You can repeat your secret saying,' his teacher told Sam. 'And only **you** will know about it.'

Sam learned from his teacher that he could use his secret saying to keep from letting the other kids win, and he wouldn't have to always be in trouble.

Sam and his teacher worked on a secret saying for Sam, and when they were done, Sam practiced repeating it over and over again. He took some deep breaths and let himself relax as he memorized his own, private, secret saying.

We can't tell you Sam's secret saying because, well . . . it's a **secret!**

But you can make up a secret saying all your own!

SmartHelp for Good 'n' Angry Kids. By Frank Jacobelli and Lynn Ann Watson
© 2009 Blackwell Publishing, ISBN 978-0-470-75802-1

You can use the lines below to begin your secret saying. Make it your own by completing it yourself or with your helper. You might want to use the rhyming words on the right, for finishing your secret saying.

Example:

No need to **stress**, 'cus . . . . . . *I'm gonna do my best*.

I know I'll be **okay**, 'cus . . . . _____.

                              (away, stay, day, play)

When I'm feeling really **tight** . . . . . . _____.

                              (flight, right, might, sight)

I'm gonna stay **calm** 'cus . . . . . . _____.

                              (mom, bomb, from, home)

I'll just let it **go** . . . . . . _____.

                              (flow, go, know, grow)

I'm staying in **control** . . . . . . _____.

                              (roll, show, stroll, blow)

Get comfortable and relaxed, take some deep breaths, and practice repeating your secret saying!

Can you think of the times when you might want to use your secret saying?

Discuss with your helper.

Rockin' Ricky

Time required: 30 minutes
Materials required: Music (MP3, CD, radio)
This is a **doing** activity.

Ricky loves all kinds of music! Rock, pop, classic rock, hip-hop, sometimes even country. He hopes to learn to play the guitar some day. Ricky feels lucky to have an MP3 player with cool headphones that seem to put his favorite music right in the middle of his brain. It sounds soooo good!

Ricky noticed that music can make him feel different kinds of feelings. Sometimes when he's feeling sad, a favorite rock song can make him feel a whole lot better.

When he's feeling mad, a soothing ballad can calm Ricky way, way down.

Whenever Ricky is feeling a little bored, just about any good song can give him all kinds of energy. And before you know it, Ricky is ready to Rock!

If you are like Ricky, your favorite music can make you feel things too.

Take a look at your favorite music and think about how the songs make you feel. You might want to listen to each one again, and really pay attention.

On the next page, write down the titles of your favorite songs in the section that describes how they make you feel. When you fell mad, sad, or bored, go to a quiet place and let your music do its magic!

SmartHelp for Good 'n' Angry Kids. By Frank Jacobelli and Lynn Ann Watson
© 2009 Blackwell Publishing, ISBN 978-0-470-75802-1

My Favorite Tunes

Makes me feel *Happy*

_____

_____

_____

Makes me feel *Calm*

_____

_____

_____

Makes me feel *'Un-bored'*

_____

_____

_____

Play your favorite tunes for your helper or a friend, and discuss.

Can you Rock Like Ricky?

Shake It Out Your Shoes

Time required: 15–20 minutes
Materials required: Music, shoes, pencil
This is a **doing** activity.

Sally likes to dance all alone in her bedroom.

Sometimes she asks her mother to dance along with her. Sally puts her favorite music on her CD player and she dances up a storm!

One day, a terrible thing happened. While riding the bus home from school, a car ran through a stoplight and hit the bus that she was riding.

Sally wasn't hurt, but two of her best friends had to go to the hospital.

After the accident, Sally had trouble sleeping, and she was getting mad all the time. Sally was just so frustrated because she felt so sad for her friends, and she was mad at the driver who wasn't paying attention to the stoplight.

Sally's mom had an idea.

'Dancing is a great way to shake out your stress and anger,' she told Sally. 'Even better, let's draw a picture on the bottom of your shoe; a picture of the car that hit your bus.'

'I've watched you dance, and I'll bet you can dance like crazy, until you wear the picture right off the bottom of your shoe!

By the time the picture wears off of your shoe, your whole body will feel better.

You can shake it out your shoes!'

Sally sharpened up a pencil and drew a big picture of the car that hit her bus, right on the sole of her shoe.

Then she turned up her favorite CD and danced for nearly a whole hour. Sally's mom danced right alongside her.

By the time she finished, her whole body was tired and relaxed, and the picture of the car was **all gone**.

SmartHelp for Good 'n' Angry Kids. By Frank Jacobelli and Lynn Ann Watson
© 2009 Blackwell Publishing, ISBN 978-0-470-75802-1

Think for a while, then use this page to write down the things that have made you stressed and angry.

_____

_____

_____

_____

Find a good pencil and get it nice and sharp. Now, find a pair of shoes that have a sole good for writing on. Write down or draw the thing (or things) you've listed, on the sole of your shoe.

Turn on the music and DANCE, DANCE, DANCE!

Can You Shake It Out Your Shoes?

WORKBOOK F

Visual-Spatial

Mike's Magic Bike

Time required: 20 minutes
Materials required: imagination
This is a **thinking** activity.

Mike got really good at pretending he had a magic bike. His bike was shiny, low, and fast, and it could fly like the wind! It could even become invisible, and when it did, Mike became invisible too.

Mike would use his magic bike to feel better about what was bothering him. Like remembering the time when his big brother, Tom, got mad at him for losing his football. Mike didn't mean to lose it. He left it lying just for a minute at the park, and when he went for it, it was gone.

Tom had gotten so mad that he hit Mike in the face and knocked out his tooth. It wasn't the tooth that hurt so much, it was that his brother would hurt him . . . really hurt him. It hurt Mike's feelings more than he could put into words.

Now when Mike feels sad about the time his brother hurt him, he imagines getting on his magic bike and racing high into the sky. He flies his bike back in time, and over the park. He swoops down on Mark's football and snatches it away before someone else takes it.

Other times, Mike imagines jumping onto his magic bike after he tells Tom that the football was taken, and together they take to the sky, Mike and his brother, and take back the stolen ball. **And no one gets hit!**

SmartHelp for Good 'n' Angry Kids. By Frank Jacobelli and Lynn Ann Watson
© 2009 Blackwell Publishing, ISBN 978-0-470-75802-1

Think of a time when you wish you had had a magic bike like Mike's.

How would you have used it?

Where does your magic bike take you?

What Bugs You?

Time required: 20 minutes
Materials required: markers
This is a **thinking** activity.

We all have things happen to us that we don't like. Some things bug us a little and some things bug us a **LOT**! And everyone is different. What bugs Tim might not bug Marcia at all. What Crystal thinks is funny, might send Taylor through the roof!

Let's use John for an example. John is 12 years old with a 6-year-old sister named Emma. John loves his little sister and most of the time he thinks she's very sweet. But every now and then Emma will go into her big brother's room when he's not there, and worst of all, Emma will get into John's **prized bug collection**. John's been collecting bugs since he was 9 and he has all kinds, shapes, and sizes. Well, John tries to be patient with Emma because he knows his little sister is, well . . . little, and she still has a lot to learn. But sometimes he is **bugged**!

A cool way to describe how you feel about something is to think about that thing, then draw a bug that matches that feeling. If something doesn't bug you at all, you might draw a *pretty butterfly*. If something bugs you a whole lot, you might draw a **big, nasty** looking bug. Here are some ideas for drawing your bugs:

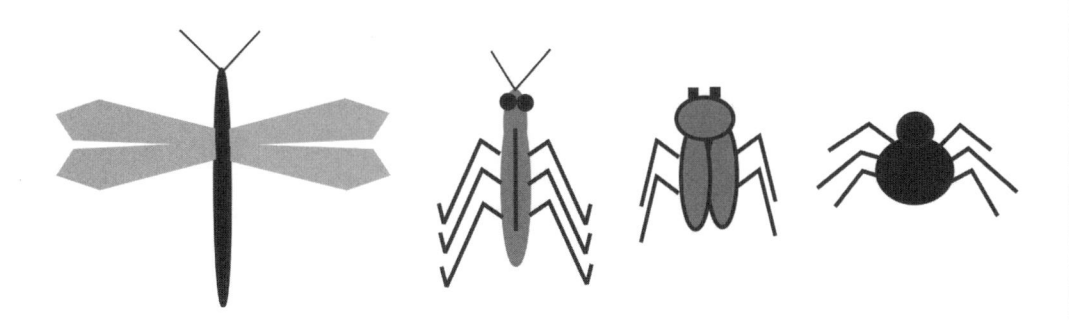

SmartHelp for Good 'n' Angry Kids. By Frank Jacobelli and Lynn Ann Watson
© 2009 Blackwell Publishing, ISBN 978-0-470-75802-1

Draw a bug for how it feels when:

You can't figure out a math problem:

You spill your milk at the dinner table:

What else bugs you?

_____ :

_____ :

_____ :

What can you do when you feel **bugged**? Talk this over with your helper.

Putting Feelings to Faces

Time required: 30 minutes
Materials required: worksheet, markers
This is a **feeling** activity.

Did you know that when you feel happy, sad, mad, scared, confused, or surprised, you are probably making a face?

In the entire world, there are just six different faces that everyone can understand.

The same faces are made by just about everybody everywhere, even by people who speak a different language. So when you can spot these faces on other people, you'll have a pretty good idea of what they are feeling.

Suppose you meet a new boy in school and he speaks only Spanish or Arabic. You might be able to figure out what he's feeling just by the look on his face.

Or say your teacher is talking to the principal on the phone but she is looking at Susie using the number 5 face. Perhaps your teacher would like for Susie to stop doing whatever it is she is doing.

SmartHelp for Good 'n' Angry Kids. By Frank Jacobelli and Lynn Ann Watson
© 2009 Blackwell Publishing, ISBN 978-0-470-75802-1

Can you match up the feeling with the face?

1.   2.   3.

4.   5.   6.

1. _____   2. _____   3. _____

4. _____   5. _____   6. _____

Why is it good to be able to put Feelings to Faces?

Discuss with your helper.

The Train that Could

Time required: 20 minutes
Materials required: markers
This is a **feeling** activity.

Willy loves trains! He lives in a house at the bottom of a steep hill near the train tracks. When there's no one to play with, Willy likes to sit on the grass and watch the trains huff and puff to make it up the hill.

After a long tough day when everything seemed to be going wrong, Willy's mom came and sat next to him on the grass, and they watched the trains together.

'See all the boxcars the locomotive is trying to pull up the hill,' his mom asked Willy, 'and see that there isn't just one locomotive, but three?'

'The train needs three locomotives because there are so many cars to pull.'

Willy learned from his mom that sometimes we are like the locomotive pulling our way through life. We have cars lined up behind us. Things like homework, bullies, best friends moving away, maybe even a grouchy teacher once in a while.

The extra locomotives are the things we do that give us strength, courage, or support for pulling our heavy load—things like getting tutoring for math, making time for football, keeping a journal, or talking with the school counselor.

Willy and his mom drew a very cool picture of a train. Inside the boxcars, Willy named (or drew) the things in his life that were sometimes hard to pull up the hill.

SmartHelp for Good 'n' Angry Kids. By Frank Jacobelli and Lynn Ann Watson
© 2009 Blackwell Publishing, ISBN 978-0-470-75802-1

In the boxcars below, write-in or draw the things that sometimes make it hard for you to climb the hill. And in the locomotives, write-in or draw the things that give you extra strength, courage, or support.

You might want to get some ideas from your helper.

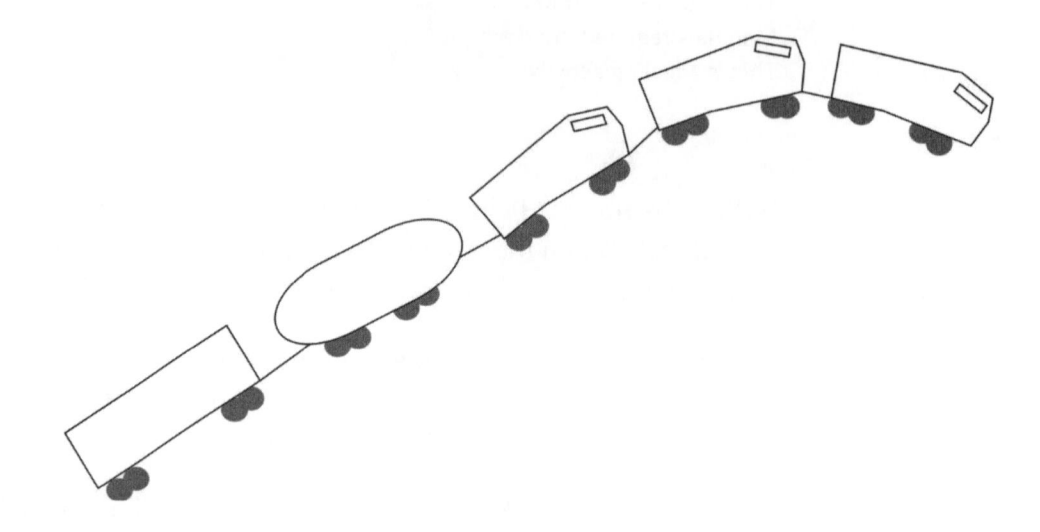

You too CAN be the train that CAN!

Vinnie on Video

Time required: 15 minutes
Materials required: video camera or digital camera, helper
This is a **doing** activity.

Vinnie watched his buddy Larry lose his cool when he didn't get picked to collect the lunch money. Larry stomped and snorted, waved his arms, and stomped his feet! Vinnie thought Larry looked pretty silly.

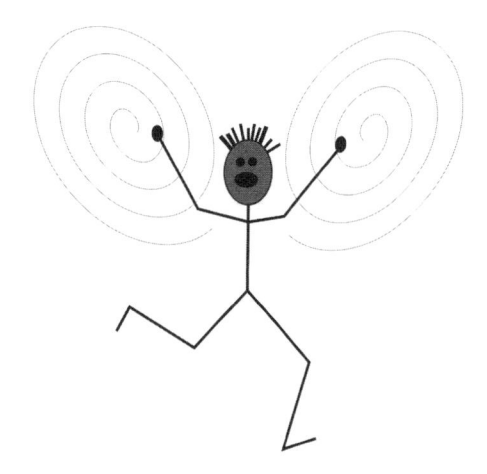

Vinnie wondered if HE looked that silly when HE lost HIS cool. Vinnie's brother had a very cool digital camera that could record video, so Vinnie asked his big brother to video him the next time he got mad.

The next day, Vinnie's mom scolded him because he didn't feed the dog and take out the garbage—his only two chores, and Vinnie lost his temper!

Vinnie's brother went for his camera and got it all on video.

SmartHelp for Good 'n' Angry Kids. By Frank Jacobelli and Lynn Ann Watson
© 2009 Blackwell Publishing, ISBN 978-0-470-75802-1

The next day, when Vinnie was calm, his brother showed him what he looked like when he was mad.

When he looked, Vinnie was amazed and more than a little embarrassed!

Would you like to know what you look like when you get mad? Ask your helper, mom, dad, brother, sister, or friend, to have their camera ready! (Helper: be sure to get parental permission.)

Picture This

Time required: 30–40 minutes
Materials required: colored markers, large sheet of poster-size paper, imagination
This is a **doing** activity.

Thinking about a very relaxing place can help us feel calm and in control. This place might be in the woods, the beach, or beside a stream. This place may be anywhere real or made up, which, when pictured in your mind, helps you to feel calm, safe, and relaxed.

First, **picture in your mind this peaceful place where you have felt (or if made up, would feel) calm and relaxed**.

Now take the picture of your calm and relaxing place from your head and **put it down on paper**, using the colors of your choice. You might want to put yourself or others in the picture, or you might not. It's fun to make your picture big and colorful.

When you are finished, **tell your helper all about your relaxing place**.

Next, your helper will teach you how to **use your drawing as a tool to help you feel more calm and relaxed**. You and your helper need to get comfortable, maybe in some cushy chairs or even on the floor with some pillows. It helps if the lights are softly dimmed.

Now that you are comfortable, your helper will show you how to **take some deep breaths**, the kind that come from a place in your body called the diaphragm. This kind of breathing will help you to feel more and more calm each time you exhale.

Next, you or your helper can hold the picture so that both of you can see it, and the two of you can softly **talk about your peaceful drawing**. The helper might have some questions about the relaxing place you have put down on paper. The helper might want to know if you could imagine hearing birds softly singing, or the sound of waves lapping at the shore. Or maybe even the sound of an unseen airplane softly humming somewhere high above.

SmartHelp for Good 'n' Angry Kids. By Frank Jacobelli and Lynn Ann Watson
© 2009 Blackwell Publishing, ISBN 978-0-470-75802-1

Once you are feeling calm and relaxed, you may want your helper to **teach you about recreating this relaxed feeling** at anytime you might wish, either by using the drawing or simply by recreating the scene in your mind.

PICTURE THIS ...

First, picture in your mind this peaceful place where you have felt (or if made up, would feel) calm and relaxed.

Now take the picture of your calm and relaxing place from your head and **put it down on paper**, using the colors of your choice.

When you've finished, tell your helper about your relaxing place.

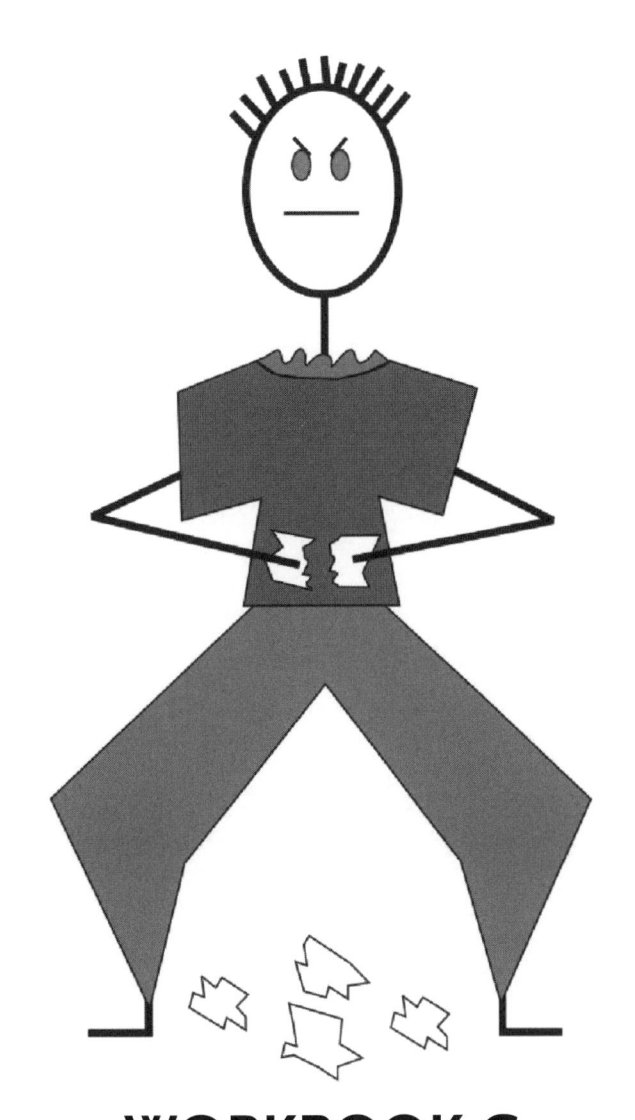

WORKBOOK G

Verbal-Linguistic

'All or Nothing' Alex

Time required: 20 minutes
Materials required: marker or pencil
This is a **thinking** activity.

Alex was a fourth-grader who got mad a lot because he had a hard time not thinking the worst!

Alex got mad when he got a 'C' on a quiz because he figured he'd NEVER get better than a C again. He got mad when his best friend Sammy couldn't stay the night, because Alex figured Sammy didn't like him anymore and would NEVER stay the night again.

With Alex, it was either all or nothing, and Alex was always getting mad because of his 'All or Nothing' thinking. Alex was embarrassed when his classmates started calling him 'All or Nothing Alex.'

Always thinking the worst was getting Alex in a lot of trouble!

SmartHelp for Good 'n' Angry Kids. By Frank Jacobelli and Lynn Ann Watson
© 2009 Blackwell Publishing, ISBN 978-0-470-75802-1

Read the situations and then circle the best answer that goes with it. **Be careful not to be an All or Nothing Alex!**

You get picked last for football	a. I'm a terrible football player and nobody likes me. b. Maybe I'm not the best football player but there are plenty of things to like about me.
You break your neighbor's window with a baseball and you have to mow his lawn for a whole month!	a. It was careless of me to break that window. I'll be more careful from now on. b. I'm nothing but a klutz and everybody knows it!
Your dad comes late to your big school play	a. My dad likes his job better than he likes me! b. My dad works so hard for us. I wish he had more time for me.
You have to go to bed and miss a special TV program	a. I wish I could see the show but I've been kind of sleepy in class. b. Mom and dad don't let me have any fun!

Are you an All or Nothing Alex?

Have a Talk With Yourself

Time required: 10–20 minutes
Materials required: worksheet, pencil or marker
This is a **thinking** activity.

Realize it or not, we all have conversations with ourselves, usually inside our heads. Often, the actions we take depend on what we say to ourselves in different situations.

One afternoon, Jason is at home with his mom and baby sister. His mom is trying to feed the baby who is a fussy eater and enjoys spitting everything out. His mother has an interview for a new job in an hour and is feeling rushed. At the same time, the smoke alarm begins to wail because of some smoke from the snack Jason is making on the stove.

His mother loses her cool and snaps at Jason, 'What is wrong with you? Can't you do anything right? I think you're trying to drive me crazy!' Jason begins to feel angry.

In the seconds that follow, Jason says some things to himself, inside his head. Some thoughts could lead Jason into a fit of anger (tossing the pan, screaming at his mother, and stomping off) or different thoughts could help him keep his cool.

SmartHelp for Good 'n' Angry Kids. By Frank Jacobelli and Lynn Ann Watson
© 2009 Blackwell Publishing, ISBN 978-0-470-75802-1

Can you decide which thoughts are which?

Have a Talk With Yourself . . .

FIT of Anger   **Keep your COOL**

Jason's thoughts:	F for fit or a **C** for cool
1. 'Wow, Mom is really stressed out about her job interview.'	_____
2. 'All she ever does is yell. I hate living here!!'	_____
3. 'I don't like being yelled at, but I didn't **mean** to make the fire alarm go off.'	_____
4. 'Maybe I could help feed the baby so Mom isn't feeling so rushed.'	_____
5. 'I'm an idiot. I can't do anything right.'	_____
6. 'I'm just a kid. I'm not perfect.'	_____

What kind of things do you say to yourself?

Discuss your answers with your helper

Keep it Simple, Sam

Time requires: 10–20 minutes
Materials required: worksheet, markers or pencil
This is a **feeling** activity.

Sam loves words! When he tells stories, he often uses words that some of his friends have never heard before. Needless to say, Sam does very well at writing papers for school, on the debate team, and when he gives an oral report in front of the class. Sam knows so many words that he can think of many different words to describe his feelings.

With all those words, sometimes Sam makes understanding feelings more complicated than they really are. Some say that there are really only five feelings, and if Sam were to list those five across the top of a blackboard, he could list a whole bunch of feelings under each, which have about the same meaning as the one at the top.

See if you can come up with five feeling words for each of Sam's feelings listed across the top. One is already completed in each column. These are to help you to get started. If you don't come up with enough words to fill all the blanks, don't feel bad, some are words we don't hear very often.

HAPPY	SAD	ANGRY	SCARED	CONFUSED
_____	_____	_____	_____	_____
_____	HURT	_____	_____	BEWILDERED
_____	_____	_____	WORRIED	_____
EXCITED	_____	_____	_____	_____
_____	_____	FRUSTRATED	_____	_____

Ask your helper if he or she knows of any other words to describe the five feelings. You might even ask if he or she has ever heard you use any other words to describe your feelings, and if so, in which column do they belong?

Why is it important for Sam to be able to name his feelings?

Discuss with your helper.

Sarah Says 'I'm Sorry'

Time required: 20 minutes
Materials required: your voice
This is a **feeling** activity.

Sarah is good at using her words!

Sarah knows so many powerful words that she can describe a camping trip to her friends and when she's finished, her friends almost feel like they'd been camping too. In fact, she's so good at using words that she hopes to be a great writer some day. Sarah really appreciates the power of words!

But of all the words that Sarah knows, the two that she feels are most powerful are 'I'm Sorry.'

When Sarah accidentally knocked another girl down on the playground, she helped the girl up and said 'I'm sorry.' Instead of being mad and wanting to fight, the girl said, 'no big deal.' (Powerful!)

When she got behind in her chores and had to cancel a sleepover, Sarah called and said 'I'm sorry.' Instead of getting mad and holding a grudge, Sarah's best friend asked, 'Do you want some help with your chores?' (Powerful!)

When Sarah interrupted her teacher by talking in class, she told her teacher, 'I'm sorry!' Instead of getting her name on the board, Sarah's teacher said, 'please don't let it happen again.' (Powerful!)

SmartHelp for Good 'n' Angry Kids. By Frank Jacobelli and Lynn Ann Watson
© 2009 Blackwell Publishing, ISBN 978-0-470-75802-1

Do you have the Power of Apology?

Write down or draw about the times when you might use the power of saying 'I'm sorry.' What might happen?

On the playground

With your brother or sister

In the classroom

With your best friend

Tell your helper about a time that you said, "I'm sorry."
What happened

What I Really Mean to Say

Time required: 10–20 minutes
Materials required: worksheet, markers or pencil, separate sheet of paper
This is a **doing** activity.

Brittany used to behave in a way that no one could understand. Not even Brittany herself. When she would get mad, Brittany would do strange things like tear up pictures of her family, run away, or throw a tantrum. Afterward, Brittany would feel embarrassed about the things she had done.

She would say to herself, 'Why didn't I use my words to say how I felt?' She decided that only when she put her feelings into words would anyone know what was bothering her, or what they could do to help.

Brittany thought long and hard, and finally figured out what it was she was really trying to say!

What I Really Mean to Say...

See if you can pair up the behavior in the left column, with what Brittany was really trying to say in the right column, by connecting them with a line...

1. Tearing up family pictures	a. 'I need some time by myself!'
2. Throwing things across the room	b. 'I hate feeling stupid in front of my friends!'
3. Slamming the door to her room	c. 'I'm so mad at you that I wish you would just go away!'
4. Yelling at her teacher	d. 'I may be little but I am strong enough to do **this**!'

Can you think of a time when you were embarrassed about and what is it that you are trying to say? Draw, make a list, or talk with your helper.

What were you really trying to say?

Carla's Cool Friend Connie

Time required: 30 minutes
Materials required: pencil or marker
This is a **doing** activity.

Carla has a new friend Connie, who came from a different school. All the kids in Connie's old school learned **a new way to be cool**. They learned that if you treat somebody like a friend, they will stop acting like an enemy. It sounds too simple to be true. But guess what? It really works!

On the first day of school, a big bully named Dina (the girls called her 'Dinamite') walked up to Connie and tried to bully her.

'Hey, new girl. Where'd you get the ugly sweater? From the garbage?'

Carla was watching, and she got so mad. She was sure Connie was going to say something mean back to Dina, and then maybe there would be a fight!

But a strange thing happened. Connie looked up at 'Dinamite' and said, 'Yeah, this old sweater has more holes than Swiss cheese. Sure is warm though!' and Connie calmly walked away smiling.

Well, Dinamite just stood there with her mouth open, not knowing what to say. She was expecting Connie to say something like, 'Oh, yeah? Well, Who asked for your opinion!' Dinamite was used to getting people mad at her, and she liked the attention. The other kids almost felt sorry for Dina. And they thought Connie was cool!

Carla learned from Connie that treating someone like a friend, even when they are acting like a bully, is much smarter than letting them get you mad. Carla hoped that all the kids would learn to make friends out of enemies, like at Connie's old school.

SmartHelp for Good 'n' Angry Kids. By Frank Jacobelli and Lynn Ann Watson
© 2009 Blackwell Publishing, ISBN 978-0-470-75802-1

Choose the best response for turning a bully into a friend!

You're so fat. I'll bet you weigh 300 pounds.
   a. At least I'm not ugly like you.
   b. Not quite. Maybe 299.

You run slower than my grandmother!
   a. Well, I guess I've never been in a big hurry.
   b. You want to make something out of it!

You miss all the easy spelling words!
   a. How would you like a punch in the nose?
   b. Hmmm, so you think I should get some extra help with my spelling?

With your helper, think up some cool responses to the bully words below.

1. You bring a peanut butter sandwich every day. Your parents must be really poor! _____
2. Your nose is so big, you look like an anteater! _____
3. You wear the same ugly shirt every day! _____

Do you know someone cool like Connie?

How about you? Can you be cool like Connie?

WORKBOOK H

Naturalist

Tip of the Iceberg

Time required: 30 minutes
Materials required: markers or pencil
This is a **thinking** activity.

An iceberg is a giant block of ice that floats in the ocean, and travels an average of 10 miles every day.

The tallest iceberg was in the North Atlantic Ocean and it was 551-feet tall. That's as tall as a 55-story building!

Maybe you've heard of the ocean liner 'Titanic' that rammed into an iceberg in 1912 and sunk in just 2 hours and 40 minutes.

The strange thing about an iceberg is that what you can see is only the tip that sticks out above the ocean, while 90% of it hides below the ocean's surface. That can be scary for ships . . . and people, too!

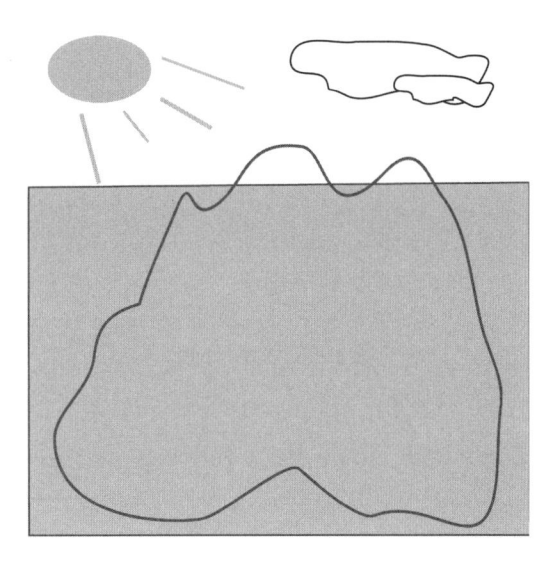

Sometimes our anger is like an iceberg. People can **see** what happens when we get angry, but there are things 'below the surface' that no one can see.

A lot of times, what's below the surface that no one can see is something that hurt us, like when someone we love has died or gone away, maybe a pet, or our parents stopped living together. Or maybe it's something that changed in our life, like starting a new school, moving away from friends, or someone in our family getting sick.

SmartHelp for Good 'n' Angry Kids. By Frank Jacobelli and Lynn Ann Watson
© 2009 Blackwell Publishing, ISBN 978-0-470-75802-1

Sometimes even **good changes** can sit below the surface and make us angry because **change is stressful**, and stress can make us angry. Things like having a baby sister or brother, moving up a grade, or having to wait for a great holiday.

Think about what things someone would see if they were to watch you when you are angry, and write or draw them in the 'tip' of the iceberg (above the ocean's surface).

Then, think about the things that you hurt about, or that cause you stress, and write or draw them in the iceberg, below the ocean's surface (as many things as you can think of).

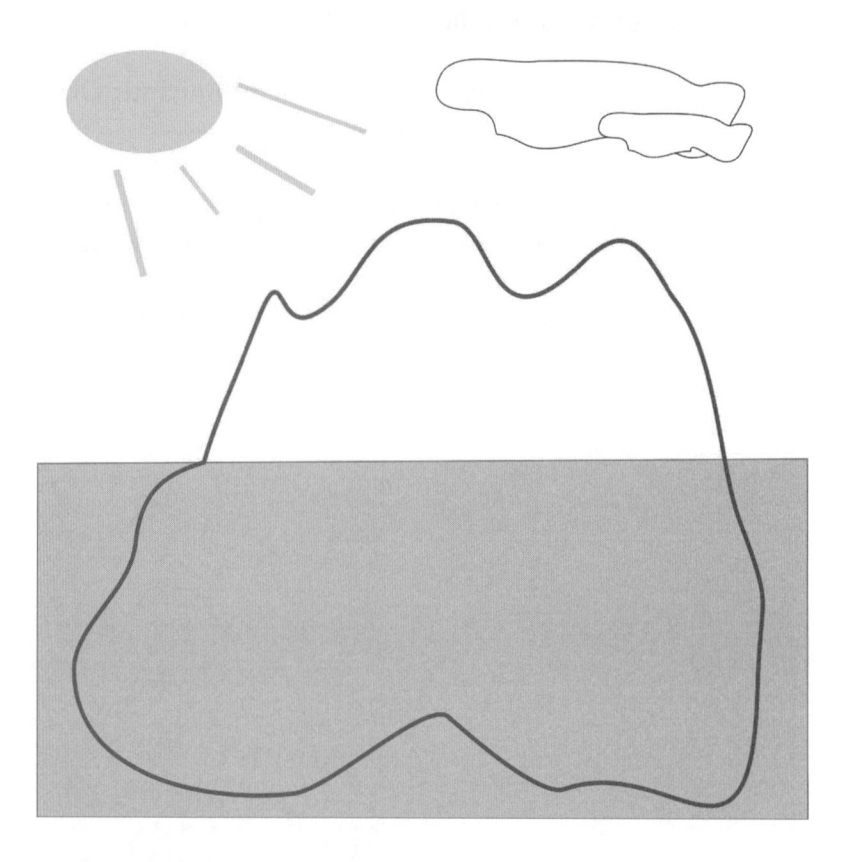

Once you know what's hurting you, talk with your helper about ways of healing your hurts.

You've already started by looking 'below the surface!'

Andrea's Ant Hill

Time required: as much as needed
Materials required: a nearby ant hill, your eyes, pencil or markers
This is a **thinking** activity.

Andrea loves the outdoors!

She has the body of an athlete and she's very good at sports. She can run, jump, and throw better than most kids, and she loves to hike, bike, and go on camping trips with her parents.

Because she's so very good at sports, Andrea thinks everyone should be just as good as her. So Andrea is always yelling at other kids to do a better job at throwing, running, catching, or kicking. Even though she's such a good player, no one ever wants to be on Andrea's team. After all, nobody likes to be yelled at!

One day in science class, Andrea learned about **ants**. She was amazed to learn that ants can carry ten times their own weight. That would be like Andrea carrying 600 pounds on her back!

She also learned that there are about 10 000 trillion ants in the world, way more than there are people. Scientists call an ant hill a 'super-organism' because of the way all the ants in an ant hill work together so well . . . just like one big super-ant!

Andrea got to thinking . . . maybe it's not so important if one person is better at something than another. Maybe what matters is how well people can work together to get something done . . . like having fun while winning the big game!

The next time she went camping, Andrea found a great big ant hill and watched the ants for hours. She drew pictures of the ants carrying food into the ant hill, stopping to touch each other whenever they passed, and of the ants themselves . . . some big, some small, some working at one thing while another worked at doing something different.

Andrea remembered her teacher saying that sometimes there are 1 000 000 ants living in one ant hill, and they all seemed to be getting along.

Andrea was very impressed!

SmartHelp for Good 'n' Angry Kids. By Frank Jacobelli and Lynn Ann Watson
© 2009 Blackwell Publishing, ISBN 978-0-470-75802-1

By learning about ants, Andrea was able to see that every person, like every ant, has a different job to do, and some are bigger, stronger, sometimes even smarter, than the others.

But what really matters is how every one is able to work together to get things done, and make the ant hill a great place to live!

After you get permission, spend some time watching the ants in an ant hill (or an ant farm) near you. (Don't get too close because some ants bite!)

Draw some of the ants that you see, doing the things that they do to make their ant hill a great place to live.

Carrying food home

Saying hello to a friend

Exploring outside the hill

Making room by carrying dirt outside

What did **you** learn about ants?

Spencer in Space

Materials needed: markers (wire, newspaper, flour and water paste, balloons, tempera paints, string for solar system model)
Time required: 30 minutes
This is a **feeling** activity.

Spencer loves to look into the sky at night, especially at the stars and the planets. Spencer's dad taught him that the stars are way, way far away, but compared to the stars, the planets aren't very far away at all.

Spencer's dad helped Spencer understand his feelings better by teaching him about the planets and how they move around the sun.

'There used to be nine planets that went around the sun, until the scientists decided that Pluto was just too small to really be a planet at all. So now there are eight. **Planets traveling around the sun are a little like feelings traveling around each one of us**. Some planets are closer to the sun than others, kind of like how sometimes we feel one way more often than another. And some planets are a lot bigger than others too, while some of our feelings are stronger than others.'

Spencer's dad showed Spencer a picture of our solar system like the one on the next page. They talked about some of the common feelings that we all feel, like **Happy, Sad, Angry, Scared**, and **Confused**. They even talked about some other kinds of feelings that we might have from time to time, like **surprised, sleepy**, and **silly**.

His dad explained that if he were Mercury, as it is the closest to the sun and the hottest, he would feel very hot and being hot makes him slow, sleepy, and tired. But Mercury is also very small, so Spencer's dad also explained that he isn't sleepy or tired a lot because he is such an active person. Spencer thought his Dad should be happier on a cooler planet like Neptune. What do you think?

SmartHelp for Good 'n' Angry Kids. By Frank Jacobelli and Lynn Ann Watson
© 2009 Blackwell Publishing, ISBN 978-0-470-75802-1

After Spencer and his dad had discussed their ideas, Spencer decided that he wanted to make a quick sketch of the planets and his feelings like the one below but that he would also like to make a real model of the solar system and paste pictures, drawings, or words on each plant to describe his feelings.

Using the picture of the solar system given here, fill in each empty planet with at least one feeling. If you decide that you want to create a model, use the suggested materials on the first page to create it.

Think about your feelings, then color-in the planets (feelings), and name the feeling that feels about the same size and distance from you, as that planet is from the sun!

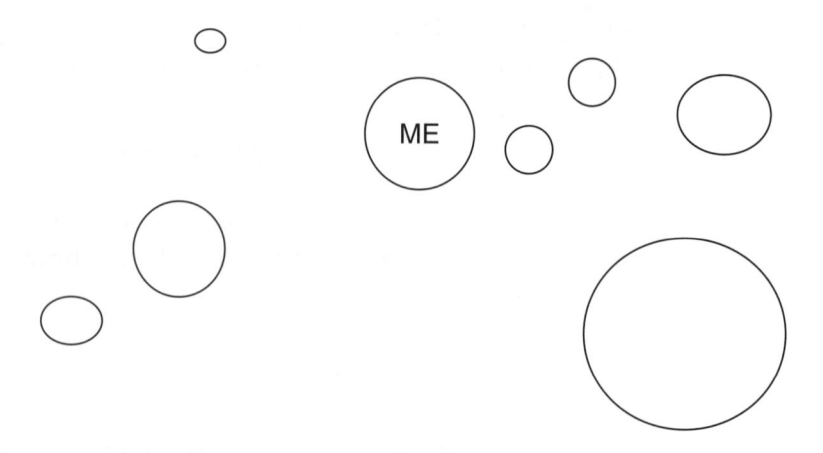

Talk about your drawing with your helper.

Vic, the Volcano

Time required: 2–40 minutes
Materials required: colored markers
This is a **feeling** activity.

Vic liked studying volcanoes. He would spend hours reading about them, looking at photographs, and drawing pictures of his own. Vic was especially interested in Mt Vesuvius and Mt Pinatubo because of their awesome power, and Mt Saint Helen's because it is so close to home.

Vic learned about the different natural materials that make up the volcano, and he learned about how those things can become transformed into the raging, incredibly powerful and out-of-control force that a volcano can sometimes unleash, often with many times the explosive power of the atomic bomb!

Vic learned that incredible heat passes through cracks from deep in the Earth's core, heating a layer of rock deep below the volcano. This melted rock called magma begins to expand and starts to rise. When the magma reaches a layer of water below the mountain, steam is created, and like a pressure cooker, the magma is pushed with great energy toward the peak of the mountain. The pressure of the super-boiling magma is awesome and it wants to escape. The mountain can no longer hold the great force and there is a great explosion, blowing the top of the mountain high into the air! The magma, after leaving the mountain, is called lava, and it flows down the mountain burning and knocking down everything in its path! The ash from the explosion goes a mile high in the air, and is carried by the wind. The ash covers everything for miles, making it hard to see and to breathe.

Vic began to realize that he could learn something else by studying volcanoes. He could learn about the times when he loses control of his anger and explodes. Vic began to think about **the heat, the cracks, the magma, the steam, the lava, and the ash**.

SmartHelp for Good 'n' Angry Kids. By Frank Jacobelli and Lynn Ann Watson
© 2009 Blackwell Publishing, ISBN 978-0-470-75802-1

Use the volcano below to describe your anger. Together with your helper, talk about and name the different things that lead to losing control of your anger. Here are some ideas to help you get started: Maybe the cracks are times when you get very tired or hungry, or maybe when you are left alone for too long. Maybe the steam is when your big brother or sister teases you, or when you are having trouble with schoolwork. Vic compared the lava to when he would throw things, and the ash to be some of the language he would use. Make your Volcano about only you!

Remember to ask your helper to help you name your:

1. Heat _____   2. Cracks _____

3. Magma _____   4. Steam _____

5. Lava _____   6. Ash _____

Label your volcano

Stella Sees Stars

Time required: 10 minutes
Materials needed: the night sky, a star chart or book about the stars
This is a **doing** activity.

Stella has two older brothers and two younger sisters. Her house is a noisy place and sometimes she feels like no one is listening to her. Sometimes Stella has to wait so long to get into the bathroom in the morning that she misses her bus. If her mom buys her favorite after-school cookies, Stella's lucky to get even one before they are all gone!

Stella loves all the twinkling stars in the night sky.

Her dad has a cool telescope and he is teaching her about the stars. Sometimes they go into the backyard and look at the stars in the quiet darkness. She learned about the red super giant star with the funny name 'Betelgeuse.' And she could hardly believe that it's 800 times bigger than the sun. It just looks smaller because it's soooooo far away from Earth . . .

Even if a spaceship could travel as fast as the light shining out of a flashlight, it would still take 427 years to reach Betelgeuse!!

But Stella's favorite star is Polaris. Polaris sits above the north pole and so it seems to stay in one place while the other stars rotate around it. Because it's always in the north, most people call Polaris 'the north star.' It's about the same distance from Earth as Betelgeuse, but Polaris is much, much smaller.

When her house gets noisy and she starts to feel tense or angry, Stella likes to go out into the backyard, sit in the cool grass, take a few deep breaths of night air, and gaze up at her favorite stars.

SmartHelp for Good 'n' Angry Kids. By Frank Jacobelli and Lynn Ann Watson
© 2009 Blackwell Publishing, ISBN 978-0-470-75802-1

Stella learned from her dad that there are billions of stars and each one has an important place in the universe. Some look brighter than others but one isn't more important than another, just different. Sometimes when Stella is feeling invisible in her big family, she thinks that they are like a *constellation*. A constellation is a group of stars in the sky that make up a kind of picture. Stella's favorite constellation is Cassiopeia because it looks like a queen in a chair.

Look up the stars on a star chart, ask your helper for help, or get a book from the library and use it to pick out some of your favorite stars and constellations. Use the space below to draw or paste pictures of your favorite stars or constellations.

Stella became so good at gazing at the stars that she could clearly imagine the night sky, even during the day, and she was able to relax.

Practice gazing at the stars when you need to relax.

You can see stars like Stella!

Felicia Finds the Forest

Time required: as much as you like
Materials required: a forest
This is a **doing** activity.

Felicia looks out the bus window and worries!

She doesn't know what she will find when she gets home from school.

Sometimes she argues with her mom, her little brother's toys are spread all over the floor, and he and his friends are running all over the house. Sometimes the only way she knows to feel calm, is to go into the woods.

When she finally gets home, it's even worse than she thought. Felicia's mom has had a bad day at work and she's a little grumpy. She insists Felicia get right to her chores and her homework, and without another word!

Once her chores and her homework are finished, Felicia heads for the woods. Felicia loves nature!

(Before you go into the woods or anywhere outside, be sure you have permission from your mom or dad.)

Once in the woods, Felicia spots a squirrel as he runs by with a nut to store for winter.

She visits her favorite snake family and notices they've grown bigger, and moved to a bigger rock down the path.

Next, Felicia goes to the little pond to see if any lily pads have blossomed since her last visit.

Before long, Felicia has noticed that all her stress and anger has melted away, and she's ready to face her problems at home.

SmartHelp for Good 'n' Angry Kids. By Frank Jacobelli and Lynn Ann Watson
© 2009 Blackwell Publishing, ISBN 978-0-470-75802-1

Felicia feels fabulous in the forest!

Think about the nature nearby your home. Even if you don't have woods nearby, maybe you have a backyard, or a nearby park or empty field. Whatever you have nearby, it's bound to have birds, bugs, flowers, plants, and other living things.

Next time you go to your **nature place**, pay attention to the many things you find that make you feel calm and happy!

Write the things you see ... and draw a picture next to it!

(Remember, you can always get help from your helper.)

_____

_____

_____

_____

Can you calm yourself with nature?

Appendix 1: Survey, Scoring Page, and Graph—Eight Strengths Survey

Please read the statements carefully and mark each one with a score of 1–3

(1 meaning never, 2 meaning sometimes, and 3 meaning always)

1. ___I'd rather listen to someone explain how to do something, than to watch them do it.
2. ___I can figure out problems easier by writing or drawing them rather than trying to do it in my head.
3. ___I like running around outside more than sitting down and playing a game.
4. ___I listen to music everyday.
5. ___People ask me if I can help them with problems.
6. ___Science and Math are more interesting to me than Reading/Literature and History.
7. ___I like being alone when I have a choice.
8. ___I like to play sports more than board games or cards.
9. ___I would much rather visit far off places than watch shows about them on television.
10. ___I am a bit of a jokester and enjoy making others laugh.
11. ___I like using a pen or pencil more than speaking.
12. ___I like working with others on a project.
13. ___I am pretty good at brainteasers, pattern games, and puzzles.
14. ___I tend to keep a lot of things to myself.
15. ___I am very comfortable in the middle of nature.
16. ___I sing or hum a lot of the time.
17. ___I am involved in team sports and am not much of a fan of doing things by myself.
18. ___I like to test things out with experiments.
19. ___I enjoy acting and dancing more than Reading and Math.
20. ___I love to verbally debate with others more than getting involved in physical competition.
21. ___I can remember something better if I put a musical beat to it.

SmartHelp for Good 'n' Angry Kids. By Frank Jacobelli and Lynn Ann Watson
© 2009 Blackwell Publishing, ISBN 978-0-470-75802-1

22. ___I get more out of using a video camera than a tape recorder.
23. ___I can see and understand the differences between the types of clouds.
24. ___I am passionate about my goals and aspirations.
25. ___During my free time, I like to play sports or physical games.
26. ___I love to look at beautiful scenery and cool pictures in books.
27. ___I am involved in social activities (clubs, sports, groups).
28. ___I can figure out answers to mathematical problems in my head without much trouble.
29. ___I would/do enjoy creating my own music.
30. ___I'd rather be outside collecting rocks or climbing a tree than being inside watching TV.
31. ___I hope to learn a lot about myself and why I am the way I am.
32. ___Words are really important to me!
33. ___I know I could invent ways to make our lives easier and better.
34. ___I have many 'close friends.'
35. ___I like to think about important life questions and/or issues.
36. ___I enjoy using big vocabulary words that sometimes others don't understand.
37. ___Biology and/or Geography are awesome subjects.
38. ___I find myself whistling, humming, or singing to a commercial I heard on TV.
39. ___My moods can often be affected by loud colors.
40. ___I have trouble sitting for long periods of time.
41. ___I work out my problems by talking to others like my family and/or friends.
42. ___After hearing a song or tune once or twice, I can usually play it, hum it, or sing it well.
43. ___I can concentrate a long time on a task that I enjoy.
44. ___I can remember what people look like easier than remembering their names.
45. ___I want to practice a new task that I have just learned, right away, using my hands.
46. ___I can easily remember and recreate bird songs and other sounds of nature.
47. ___Reading/Literature, Social Studies, and History are very interesting to me.
48. ___I am very organized and I can help other people organize their time.
49. ___I can see the patterns or steps in complicated tasks or projects.
50. ___I am different from the rest of the 'crowd.'
51. ___I often use my hands or body language when I am trying to describe something.
52. ___I am a leader to others.
53. ___Protecting nature is extremely important to me.
54. ___I play an instrument or believe I would be good at it if I did.
55. ___I have an easy time imagining interesting situations or making up stories in my head.
56. ___I enjoy puzzles or other word games.
57. ___It's important to me that things around me are neat and organized.
58. ___Great ideas pop into my head while I am doing some sort of physical activity.

59. ___I like learning the names of different trees, plants, and flowers.
60. ___I like to work alone without distractions.
61. ___Music affects my moods and I can easily express myself through the use of music.
62. ___I love to use my imagination!
63. ___I love going out to crowded events.
64. ___I can express myself very well by writing things down.

To score your questionnaire, follow these basic steps. After each **Strength Heading**, write each score from the survey above the question **number**, then add the scores to get the grand total. Take each of the totals and graph them on the 8 Strengths Graph. You may color in each column to be able to "see" which may be your best learning styles. Using this information, you and your helper may choose the activity sections that utilize your strengths to help you deal with a particular situation.

Logical-Mathematical $\frac{\ }{6} + \frac{\ }{13} + \frac{\ }{18} + \frac{\ }{28} + \frac{\ }{33} + \frac{\ }{48} + \frac{\ }{49} + \frac{\ }{57} = $ _____

Bodily-Kinesthetic $\frac{\ }{3} + \frac{\ }{8} + \frac{\ }{19} + \frac{\ }{25} + \frac{\ }{40} + \frac{\ }{45} + \frac{\ }{51} + \frac{\ }{58} = $ _____

Intrapersonal $\frac{\ }{7} + \frac{\ }{14} + \frac{\ }{24} + \frac{\ }{31} + \frac{\ }{35} + \frac{\ }{43} + \frac{\ }{50} + \frac{\ }{60} = $ _____

Musical-Rhythmic $\frac{\ }{4} + \frac{\ }{16} + \frac{\ }{21} + \frac{\ }{29} + \frac{\ }{38} + \frac{\ }{42} + \frac{\ }{54} + \frac{\ }{61} = $ _____

Visual-Spatial $\frac{\ }{2} + \frac{\ }{11} + \frac{\ }{22} + \frac{\ }{26} + \frac{\ }{39} + \frac{\ }{44} + \frac{\ }{55} + \frac{\ }{62} = $ _____

Interpersonal $\frac{\ }{5} + \frac{\ }{12} + \frac{\ }{17} + \frac{\ }{27} + \frac{\ }{34} + \frac{\ }{41} + \frac{\ }{52} + \frac{\ }{63} = $ _____

Verbal-Linguistic $\frac{\ }{1} + \frac{\ }{10} + \frac{\ }{20} + \frac{\ }{32} + \frac{\ }{36} + \frac{\ }{47} + \frac{\ }{56} + \frac{\ }{64} = $ _____

Naturalist $\frac{\ }{9} + \frac{\ }{15} + \frac{\ }{23} + \frac{\ }{30} + \frac{\ }{37} + \frac{\ }{46} + \frac{\ }{53} + \frac{\ }{59} = $ _____

8 Strengths Graph

24								
23								
22								
21								
20								
19								
18								
17								
16								
15								
14								
13								
12								
11								
10								
9								
8								
7								
6								
5								
4								
3								
2								
1								
	Logical - Mathematical	Bodily - Kinesthetic	Intra- personal	Musical - Rhythmic	Visual - Spatial	Inter- personal	Verbal - Linguistic	Naturalist

Appendix 2: Answer Guide

▶ Workbook A

This thing called anger

1. normal part of who we are
2. pleasant
3. d
4. adventure

Figuring out who I am

I AM COOL

Crack the cool code

68101 = STOP
9121432 = RELAX
345 = AND
8111347 = THINK

▶ Workbook D

Chuck checks it out

a
b
a

SmartHelp for Good 'n' Angry Kids. By Frank Jacobelli and Lynn Ann Watson
© 2009 Blackwell Publishing, ISBN 978-0-470-75802-1

Sizzling Simon

c
c
a

▶ Workbook F

Putting feeling to faces

1. Surprised
2. Sad
3. Happy
4. Scared
5. Mad
6. Confused

▶ Workbook G

All or nothing Alex

b
a
b
a

Have a talk with yourself

1. c
2. f
3. c
4. c
5. f
6. c

What I really mean to say

1. c
2. d
3. a
4. b

Carla's cool friend Connie

1. b
2. a
3. b

Bibliography

Achenbach, T., McConaughty, S., and Howell, C. 'Child/adolescent behavioral and emotional problems: Implications for cross-informant correlations for situational specificity.' *Psychological Bulletin*, 1987, vol. **101**: 213–232.

Add.about.com. (a New York Times company). 'Famous people with attention deficit disorder.' 2007.

Amen, D. *Change Your Brain Change Your Life*. Three Rivers Press: New York, 1998.

Amen, D. *Healing ADD: The Breakthrough Program that Allows you to See and Heal the 6 Types of ADD*. Berkley Publishing Group: New York, 2001.

Armstrong, T. *Seven Kinds of Smart*. Plume: New York, 1993.

Armstrong, T. *The Myth of the ADD Child: 50 Ways to Improve Your Child's Behavior and Attention Span without Drugs, Labels, or Coercion*. Plume: New York, 1997.

Baker, L., Jacobson, K., Raine, A., Lozano, D., and Bezdjian, S. 'Genetics and environment bases of childhood antisocial behavior: A multi-informant twin study.' *Journal of Abmormal Psychology*, 2007, vol. **116**, No. 2: 219–235.

Bandura, A., Ross, D., and Ross, S.A. Transmission of aggressions through imitation of aggressive models. *Journal of Abnormal and Social Psychology*, 1961, vol. **63**: 572–582.

Benis, A. *Toward Self and Sanity: On the Genetics of the Human Character*. Psychological Dimensions: New York, 1985, eBook, revised 2004.

Barkley, R. *Attention-Deficit Hyperactivity Disorder*. Guilford Press: New York, 1998.

Bar-On, R., Trandel, D., Denburg, N., and Bechara, A. 'Exploring the neurological substrate of emotional and social intelligence.' *Brain: A Journal of Neurology*, 2003, vol. **126**, No. 8: 1790–1800.

Bipolar disorder statistics. Depression and Bipolar Alliance (Internet site), 2006.

Bloom, P. How children learn the meaning of words. *Behavioral and Brain Sciences*, 2001, vol. **24**: 1095–1103.

Borba, M. *Character Builders: Positive Attitudes and Peacemaking for Primary Grades*. Jalmar PR, 2001.

Campbell, D. *The Mozart Effect*. Avon: New York, 1997.

Carter, L. *Destructive Emotions*. Jossey-Bass: San Francisco, CA, 2003.

Children's mental health facts. Children and adolescents with conduct disorder. SAMHSA's National Mental Health Information Center, 2003.

Clark, J., Dawson, C., and Bredehoft, D. *How Much Is Enough?* Marlowe and Company: New York, 2004.

Coccaro, E., Bergeman, C., Kavoussi, R., and Seroczynski, A. Heritability of aggression and irritability: A twin study of the Buss-Durkee Aggression Scales in adult male twins. *Biological Psychiatry*, 1997, vol. **41**: 273–284.

Cozolino, L. *The Neuroscience of Psychotherapy*. W.W. Norton: New York, 2002.

Crawford, E. 'The law of love.' *The Rosocurian Digest*, May, 1973.

Dalai Lama and Goleman, D. *Destructive Emotions*. Bantam Books: New York, 2003.

Damasio, A. *Descartes Error*. Quill: New York, 2000.

Diagnostic and Statistical Manual, Vol. **4**, Text Revised. American Psychiatric Association, 2000.

Dorba, M. *Building Moral Intelligence*. Jossey-Bass: San Francisco, CA, 2001.

Duffy, F. (editorial) Journal of Electroencephalography, January, 2000.

Fiero, J. Anger. *'Ethics.' Revised edition*, Vol. 1.

Freeman, J., Epston, D., and Lobovitz, D. *Playful Approaches to Serious Problems*. W.W. Norton: New York, 1997.

Fuller, C. *Unlocking Your Child's Learning Potential*. Pinon: Colorado Springs, 1994.

Gardner, H. *Frames of Mind: The Theory of Multiple Intelligences*. Basic Books: New York, 1983.

SmartHelp for Good 'n' Angry Kids. By Frank Jacobelli and Lynn Ann Watson
© 2009 Blackwell Publishing, ISBN 978-0-470-75802-1

Gardner, H. *Multiple Intelligences: New Horizons*. Basic Books: New York, 2006.

Gattuso, J. *A Course in Love*. Penguin Putnam: New York, 1998.

Glasser, H. and Easley, J. *Transforming the Difficult Child*. Nurtured Heart Publications: Tucson, AZ, 1998.

Glasser, H. *101 Reasons to Avoid Ritalin Like the Plague*. Nurtured Heart Publications: Tucson, 2005.

Goldberg, E. *The Executive Brain: Frontal Lobes and the Civilized Mind*. University Press: New York, 2001.

Golden, D. 'Building a better brain.' *Life*. July 1994, 62–70.

Goldstein, A., Glick, B., and Gibbs, J. *Aggression Replacement Therapy*. Research Press: Champaign, IL, 1998.

Goleman, D. *Emotional Intelligence*. Bantam: New York, 1995.

Gomez, J. and Michaelis, R. An assessment of burnout in human services providers. *Journal of Rehabilitation*, 1995, vol. **61**: 23.

Gould, E., Reeves, A.J., Graziano, M.S., and Gross, C.G. Neurogenesis in the cortex of adult primates. *Science*, 1999, vol. **286**, No. 5439: 548–552.

Greenhill, L., Halperin, J., and Abikoff, H. Stimulant medications. *Journal of American Adolescent Psychiatry*, 1999, vol. **38**, No. 5: 503–512.

Hallowel, E. and Ratey, J. *Driven to Distraction*. Touchstone: New York, 1995.

Hamm, R.J., Temple, M.D., O'Dell, D.M., Pike, P.R., and Lyeth, B.G. Exposure to environmental complexity promotes recovery of cognitive function after brain injury. *Journal of Neurotrauma*, 1996, vol. **13**, No.1: 41–47.

Hammond, C. Behavioural Neurotherapy Clinic, 2005, www.adhd.com.au/neurotherapy.htm

Harlow, J. Recovery from the passage of an iron bar through the head. *Publications of the Massachusetts Medical Society*, 1868, vol. **2**: 327–347, Passage of an iron bar through the head. *Boston Medical and Surgical Journal*, 1848–1849, vol. **39**: 389.

Hughes, P. Anger. *Encyclopedia of Ethics*, vol. **1** (2nd edition). Rutledge Press, 2001.

Jacobelli, F. and Watson, L.A. *ADHD Drug Free: Natural Alternatives and Practical Exercises for Helping Your Child Focus*. Amacom: New York, 2008.

Johnson, K. *Trauma in the Lives of Children*. Hunter House, 1989.

Johnson, L.D. *Get on the Peace Train: A Journey from Anger to Harmony*. Head Acre Publishing: Salt Lake City, UT, 2004.

Josephson Institute of Ethics. Resources-Quote Library-"Quote Unquote", 2007.

Kalman, I. *Bullies to Buddies*. The Wisdom Pages: Staten Island, 2005.

Kanel, K.A. *A Guide to Crisis Intervention* (3rd edition). Thomson Brooks/Cole, 2006.

Kemp, S. and Strongman, K. Anger theory and management: A historical analysis. *American Journal of Psychology*, 1995, vol. **108**, No. 3: 397–417.

Kemperman, G., Kuhn, H.G., and Gage, F.H. More hippocampal neurons in adult mice living in an enriched environment. *Nature*, 1997, vol. **386**, No. 6624: 493–495.

Kluger, K. 'Are we giving our kids too many drugs?' *Time*. October, 2003.

Lazear, D. *Multiple Intelligence Approaches to Assessment*. Zephyr Press: Tucson, AZ, 1994a.

Lazear, D. *Seven Pathways of Learning*. Zephyr Press: Tucson, AZ, 1994b.

LeDoux, J. Emotions memory and the brain. *Scientific American*, 1994, vol. **270**: 50–57.

LeDoux, J. *The Synaptic Self*. Viking Penguin: New York, 2002.

Lewis, T., Amini, F., and Lannon, R. *A General Theory of Love*. Random House: New York, 2000.

Lickona, T. *Educating for Character*. Bantam: New York, 1991.

Lorenz, K. *On Aggression*. Rutledge Classics, 2002.

Lubar, J. *Quantitative Electroencephalographic Analysis (QEEG) Databases for Neurotherapy: Description, Validation, and Application*. The Haworth Medical Press: New York, 2003.

Martin, R. and Dahlen, E. Irrational beliefs and the experience and expression of anger. *Journal of Rational-Emotive and Cognitive-Behavioral Therapy*, 2004, vol. **22**: 3–20.

Mckay, M., Rogers, P., and McKay, J. *When Anger Hurts: Quieting the Storm Within*. New Harbinger Publishing: Oakland, 2003.

Messer, M. *Managing Anger: Handbook of Proven Techniques*. The Anger Institute: Chicago, 2001.

Neiser, U., Boodoo, G., Bouchard, T., Boykin, A., Brody, N., Ceci, S., Halpern, D., Loehlin, J., Perloff, R., and Urbina, S. Intelligence: knowns and unknowns. *American Psychologist*, 1996, vol. **51**: 77–101.

Palladino, L.J. *Dreamers, Discoverers and Dynamos: How to Help the Child who is Bright, Bored, and Having Problems in School*. Ballantine Publishing: New York, 1999.

Papolos, D. and Papolos, J. *The Bipolar Child* (3rd edition). Broadway Books: New York, 2006.

Payne, R. *A Framework for Understanding Poverty*. Aha Process: Highlands, 2005.

Peck, M. *The Road Less Traveled*. Simon and Schuster: New York, 1978.

Perry, B. Neurodevelopment and the neurophysiology of trauma. *APSAC Advisor*, 1993, vol. **6**, No.1–2: 1–18.

Perry, B. *Maltreated Children: Experience, Brain Development and the Next Generation*. Norton: New York, 1995.

Perry, B. Helping traumatized children, 1999, www.childtrauma.org.

Perry, B. 'Safe from the Start' (video). California Attorney General's Office, 2004.

Perry, B. Aggression and violence: the neurobiology of experience, 2007a, http://teacher.scholastic.com.

Perry, B. The impact of abuse and neglect on the developing brain, 2007b, teacher.scholastic.com.

Phelan, T. *1-2-3 Magic: Effective Discipline for Children 2–12* (3rd edition). ParentsMagic: Glen Ellyn, 2003.

Pines, A. and Maslach, C. Characteristics of staff burnout in mental health settings. *Hospital and Community Psychiatry*, 1978, vol. **29**: 223–233.

Raine, A. Annotation: The role of prefrontal deficits, low autonomic arousal, and early health factors in the development of antisocial and aggressive behavior. *Journal of Child Psychology and Psychiatry*, 2002, vol. **43**: 417–434.

Plumb, C. 'Packing parachutes.' The United States Naval Academy Online Community, 2001.

Reiff, M. *ADHD: A Complete and Authoritative Guide*. American Academy of Pediatrics, 2004.

Ruben, D.H. *Bratbusters: Say Goodbye to Tantrums and Disobedience*. Skidmore-Roth Publishers: El Paso, TX, 1992.

Ruben, D.H. *Parent Empowerment: Counseling Parents in Positive Child-Rearing Practices*. Cross Country University, 2002.

Ruiz, D. *The Four Agreements*. Amber-Allen Publishing: San Rafael, CA, 1997.

Saarni, C. *The Development of Emotional Competence*. Guilford Press: New York, 1999.

Salovey, P. and Sluyter, D. *Emotional Development and Emotional Intelligence*. Basic Books: New York, 1997.

Schiraldi, G. *The Anger Management Sourcebook*. Contemporary Books, 2003.

Semmelroth, C. and Smith, D. *The Anger Habit*. Writer's Showcase: New York, 2000.

Siegel, D. *The Developing Mind*. Guilford Press: New York, 1999.

Sims, D. and Franklin, A. *The Other Side of Grief*. Grief Inc, Louisville, KY, 2003.

Spackman, M.P. How to do things with emotions. *Journal of Mind and Behavior*, 2002, vol. **23**, No. 4, 393–412.

Sparks, P., Simon, G., Katon, W., Altman, L., Ayers, G., and Johnson, R. An outbreak of illness among aerospace workers. *Western Journal of Medicine*, 1990, vol. **153**: 28.

Stevens, E. *Oppositional Defiant Disorder, Conduct Disorder, & the Role of Attachment*. Eau claire: MEDS-PDN, 2007.

Swindoll, C. *The Strength of Character: 7 Essential Traits of a Remarkable Life*. Thomas Nelson Pub, 2007.

Wagemaker, H. *Psychiatric Medications and Our Children: A Parent's Guide*. Ponte Vedra Publishing: Ponte Vedra, 2003.

Wells, R.H. *Breakthrough Strategies to Teach and Counsel Troubled Kids*, Youth Change, 1993.

Williams, E. *Presenter on Disruptive, Unmotivated, Struggling at Risk Students*, MEDS-PDN, 2007.

Who can explain the mystery of 'I'? Maybe 'them'—twins, those doppelzangers that fascinate us all, *Psychology Today*, August, 1997.

Index

Note: Entries in *italics* refer to worksheets.

abstract thinking 40
acting out 23
Adderall 33
adolescents 30, 35
aggression 15, 16, 17
alcohol 23
'All or Nothing' Alex 165
Amen Clinic 8, 11
Amen, Daniel 8, 11
American Academy of Pediatrics 31
American Psychological Association 6
Amphetamine–Dextroamphetamine 33
Andrea's Ant Hill 181
anger 1, 12
anger management 6, 7, 8, 14
apathy 21
Aristotle 5
Armstrong, Thomas 33, 34
ASB factor 20
Asperger's Syndrome 29
Attention Deficit Hyperactivity Disorder 29, 32, 33, 34, 35
   combined type 33
   predominantly hyperactive type 33
   predominantly inattentive type 33
Autism Spectrum Disorder 29

Baker, Laura 20
Bandura, Albert 31
Barkley, Russell 34
Barnum, P.T. 11
behavior analysis 40
behavior specialist 41, 42
Ben Beats the Blahs 119
Benis, A.M. 21
Bipolar Disorder 35
   mania 35
   mixed-symptom states 35
   onset 35
   rapid cycling 35
Bobby Keeps the Beat 141
Bobo Doll experiment 31
Bonnie Can Balance 91
Borba, Michelle 21
brain
   amygdala 9, 10, 12
   brainstem 32
   corpus callosum 12
   development 12
   frontal lobe 1
   high road 10
   hippocampus 9, 10
   low road 9
   neocortex 9, 10
   prefrontal cortex 1, 12
   'reptilian' 9
   temporal lobe 10, 11, 12
   thalamus 9
brain-based 31
Brenda in a Bag 109
Buddhism 8
bullying 3
burnout 39, 48–50

caffeine 47
Cage, Phineas 11, 12
Carla's Cool Friend Connie 175
Celiac Disease 69
cerebral blood flow 11
character 5, 19, 21, 22, 24, 25, 26, 27
charity 16
Child Trauma Academy 31
Children's Success Foundation 34
Christianity 5
Chuck Checks it Out 133
Churchill, Winston 51
civil rights 13
Cognitive Behavioral Therapy 36
Color You Calm 115
comfort foods 47
compassionate-out 29, 30
Conduct Disorder 29, 36
consequences 9, 12, 13
coping strategies 22
Counting to Calm 99
Cozolino, Louis 8
Crack the Cool Code 89
Cylert 33

Dalai Lama 8
deep breathing 38
Depakote 66
depression 16
Depression and Bipolar Support Alliance 35
despair 21
Dexedrine 33
Dextroamphetamine 33
divorce 7
Don't Blow It 103
drugs 23
DSM-IV-TR 30, 31, 32, 33

Eight (8) Pillar Graph 73
Einstein, Albert 51
Ekman, Paul 8
emotion 6, 7, 8, 10, 13
emotional regulation 10
energy-challenged 45, 46
environment 41, 42, 50
executive function 1, 46

family therapy 40, 42
fatigue 47
feeding the good wolf 24–5
Felicia Finds the Forest 189
Fetal Alcohol Effect (Spectrum Disorder) 65
Fiero 5
fight or flight 9
Figuring Out Who I Am 87
Fish oil 47
Frank Feels the Fire 97
Freud, Sigmund 16
frustration 22, 24
Fuller, Cheri 52

Galen 5
Gandhi, Mahatma 53
Gardner, Howard 51, 53–5
Gattuso, Joan 25
genetics 19, 20, 21
Glasser, Howard 34
gluten 69
Goldberg, Elkhonon 8
golden compass 20
Goleman, Daniel 8
Goodship, Daphne 19
gratification 22, 24
Greenberg, Mark 10
grief 7

Hannah Asks for Help 127
Have a Talk With Yourself 167
head start 62
Herbert, Barbara 19
hitting 46
Horney, Karen 21
hostility 15
Hume, David 16
humor 45
hurt 7, 13
hyperactive 29, 32, 33, 35

I, I, Irene 125
individual learning 1, 2, 3
Individualized Education Plan 63
Inge, William 5
IQ test 69

Johnson, Lynn 8

Kalman, Izzy 17, 44, 45
Kant, Immanuel 5
Keep it Simple, Sam 169

labeling of kids 29, 33
language 53, 55
Larry's Lyrics to Live By 137
Lazear, David 52, 53, 55
Leakey, Richard 6
learning disability 40
learning style aware 2
learning style survey 3, 73, 191
learning styles 1, 2, 3
    bodily-kinesthetic 2, 52
    interpersonal 53, 121
    intrapersonal 52, 107
    logical-mathematical 79

musical-rhythmic 53
naturalist 54
verbal-linguistic 2, 53
visual-spatial 2, 53
Ledoux, Joseph 8
level system 42
lithium 35
Lorenz, Konrad 16, 17
lying 36

Machiavelli 53
malnutrition 69
managed care 50
manhood 6
marijuana 23
marriage and family 41
matching 43
Me in the Mirror 83
medication 30, 31, 33, 34, 35, 36
mediocrity 21
Mendelian genetics 21
Messer, Mitchell 7, 8
Methylphenidate 33
middle-class 26, 27
Mike's Magic Bike 151
Milieu 42
Mirroring Matthew 129
moral code 21
music 48
My Three Favorite Things 113

narcissism 21
National Institute of Mental Health 20
naturalist learning style 54
neglect 12
neurobiology 32
neuroplasticity 8
neurotherapy 33
neurotics 25
non-public school 65
NPA Theory of Personality 21
numbing-down 34
nurturing 25

Omega 3, 47
Oppositional Defiant Disorder 29

Panic Disorder 49
Pasteur, Louis 51
Paul Hits the Wall 105
Peck, M. Scott 25
perfectionism 21
Perry, Bruce 9, 12
Pervasive Developmental Disorder 29
Phelan, Thomas 42
Picture This 161
Plasticity 8
Playing it Cool 131
Plumb, Charles 27
Post-traumatic Stress Disorder 65
poverty 67
Pemoline 33
privileges 42
psychologist 64
psychotherapy 25
Putting Feelings to Faces 155

Rappin' Randy Raps it Out 139
Rational Psychology Association of Munich 34
Ray on the Rise 111
recovery 24
reinforcement 44
relearning 10
religion 25
responsibility 22, 23, 25, 26, 27
Ritalin 33
road rage 3
Rockhound Rhonda 101
Rockin' Ricky 145
role-models 20
Ruben, Douglas 43
Ruiz, Don Miguel 25, 26

Sam's Secret Saying 143
Sarah Says 'I'm Sorry' 171
schizophrenia 19
school shootings 3
seizures 11
self-esteem 1
self-soothing 1
Semmelroth, Carl 17
Seneca 5, 15
sermon on the Mount 16
severely emotionally disturbed 42
sex 22, 23
sexual abuse 7
Shake It Out Your Shoes 147
short-attention-span-culture 34
Siegel, Daniel 8
Sims, Darcy 7
Single Photon Emission Computerized Tomography (SPECT) 11, 12
Sizzling Simon 123
SmartHelp 1, 3
Smith, Donald 17
Snack-food for Thought 95
Spencer in Space 183
spirituality 25
stamina 47
Stanford Achievement Test 55
Stanford Middle School 54

stealing 36
Stella Sees Stars 187
story-telling 21
suicidal ideation 61
survival 6, 9, 12, 13
Swindoll, Charles 9

tantrums 35
task-specific 14
temptation 21, 25
The Train that Could 157
therapist 41
thinking, feeling, doing interplay 75
This Thing Called Anger 81
threat 6, 9, 13, 14
three poisons 8
three second pause 9
time-out 42–3
Tip of the Iceberg 179
tobacco 36
trauma 12
tremor 36
truancy 36
twin studies 19

use-dependent 12

vengeance 16
Vic, the Volcano 185
Vinnie on Video 159
violence 7, 12, 16, 17
visual imagery 77

Wagemaker, Herbert 35
Walt Learns to Wait 85
What Bugs You? 153
What I Really Mean to Say 173
When Gary Gets Going 117
Wilson, Woodrow 51
World Health Organization 30
wrestling 31

yoga 48

zero-tolerance 44

35 women x 2
8 10 women

$\frac{7x}{2L} + T = \ddot{x}$

$\frac{\ddot{x}}{2L} + \frac{7}{280}$